Truth for Today

a chapter-by-chapter devotional through the New Testament

Truth for Today

a chapter-by-chapter devotional through the New Testament

Dr. Neal Jackson

Neal Jackson

Phil 1:21

CreateSpace Independent Publishing Platform
© 2015 Neal Jackson
ISBN-13: 978-1519586353
ISBN-10: 1519586353

Cover Design: Shutterstock, Tracy Jackson
Interior Design: Tracy Jackson
Editing: Merrick J Stemen

One of my settled convictions as a pastor is the necessity of getting people to spend time daily reading their Bibles. Since it is the Word that gives life, John 6:63, then one of my great tasks as a pastor is not just to preach the Word and live the Word but to persuade those under my care to be daily in the Word. One of the secrets to the incredible growth spiritually and numerically of the early church was the Word of God increasing in their lives, Acts 6:7, Acts 12:24, Acts 19:20. My hope and prayer for this book is that God would use it bring life as His word increases in your life.

We have laid out this book to be read along with your daily devotions Monday through Friday through the New Testament. If you will read one chapter a day Monday through Friday you will read through the entire New Testament in a year. As I read my Bible daily whatever truth the Holy Spirit prompts me with, I make notes about it or a short outline so it's easier to remember. That's what you will find in this book, my thoughts, ramblings, and mostly outlines. Each day I have jotted down a short outline of a verse or group of verses that spoke to me as I was reading my Bible. My hope is that you will do the same. As you are reading through each chapter make your own outline or improve on my outline. Let us learn and grow together as we study God's Word. Many blessings to you as you "study to shew yourself approved unto God."

Neal Jackson

I. Joseph was a Devout Man

Mattew 1:19 "Then Joseph her husband, **being a just man**, and not willing to make her a publick example, was minded to put her away privily."

II. Joseph was a Discerning Man

Mattew 1:19 "Then Joseph her husband, being a just man, and not willing to make her a publick example, **was minded to put her away privily.**"

III. Joseph was a Deliberate Man

Matthew 1:20 "**But while he thought on these things,** behold, the angel of the Lord appeared unto him in a dream, saying, Joseph, thou son of David, fear not to take unto thee Mary thy wife: for that which is conceived in her is of the Holy Ghost."

IV. Joseph was a Devoted Man

Matthew 1:24 "Then Joseph being raised from sleep **did as the angel of the Lord had bidden him,** and took unto him his wife:"

Joseph was committed to his God. Let's follow his example!!

I. Wisemen sought after Christ

Matthew 2:1-2 "Now when Jesus was born in Bethlehem of Judaea in the days of Herod the king, behold, there came wise men from the east to Jerusalem, [2]Saying, Where is he that is born King of the Jews? for we have seen his star in the east, and are come to worship him."

II. Wisemen Submitted to Christ

Matthew 2:11 "And when they were come into the house, they saw the young child with Mary his mother, and fell down, and worshipped him:"

III. Wisemen Sacrificed for Christ

Matthew 2:11 "...they presented unto him gifts; gold, and frankincense, and myrrh."

We would be wise to follow the example of these wise men!!

I. The Preaching of John the Baptist

Matthew 3:2 "And saying, Repent ye: for the kingdom of heaven is at hand."

II. The Presentation of John the Baptist

Matthew 3:4 "And the same John had his raiment of camel's hair, and a leathern girdle about his loins; and his meat was locusts and wild honey."

III. The Parishioners of John the Baptist

Matthew 3:5 "Then went out to him Jerusalem, and all Judaea, and all the region round about Jordan"

IV. The Persecution of John the Baptist

Matthew 3:7 "But when he saw many of the Pharisees and Sadducees come to his baptism, he said unto them, O generation of vipers, who hath warned you to flee from the wrath to come?"

V. The Purpose of John the Baptist

Matthew 3:11-12 "I indeed baptize you with water unto repentance: but he that cometh after me is mightier than I, whose shoes I am not worthy to bear: he shall baptize you with the Holy Ghost, and with fire: [12]Whose fan is in his hand, and he will throughly purge his floor, and gather his wheat into the garner; but he will burn up the chaff with unquenchable fire."

John the Baptist lived for Jesus. Let's follow his example!!

I. Jesus was Tempted with his Desires

Matthew 4:2-3 "And when he had fasted forty days and forty nights, he was afterward an hungered. [3]And when the tempter came to him, he said, If thou be the Son of God, command that these stones be made bread."

II. Jesus was Tempted with his Decisions

Matthew 4:6 "And saith unto him, If thou be the Son of God, cast thyself down: for it is written, He shall give his angels charge concerning thee: and in their hands they shall bear thee up, lest at any time thou dash thy foot against a stone."

III. Jesus was tempted with His Devotion

Matthew 4:8-9 "Again, the devil taketh him up into an exceeding high mountain, and sheweth him all the kingdoms of the world, and the glory of them; [9]And saith unto him, All these things will I give thee, if thou wilt fall down and worship me."

Jesus defeated Temptation by relying on God's Word!!

Matthew 4:4 "But he answered and said, **It is written**, Man shall not live by bread alone, but by every word that proceedeth out of the mouth of God."

Matthew 4:7 "Jesus said unto him, **It is written** again, Thou shalt not tempt the Lord thy God."

Matthew 4:10 "Then saith Jesus unto him, Get thee hence, Satan: for **it is written**, Thou shalt worship the Lord thy God, and him only shalt thou serve."

I. Shake the Salt on a Decaying World

Matthew 5:13 "Ye are the salt of the earth: but if the salt have lost his savour, wherewith shall it be salted? it is thenceforth good for nothing, but to be cast out, and to be trodden under foot of men."

II. Shine the Light on a Dark World

Matthew 5:14 "Ye are the light of the world. A city that is set on an hill cannot be hid."

III. Share the Love with a Depraved World

Matthew 5:16 "Let your light so shine before men, that they may see your good works, and glorify your Father which is in heaven."

You can make a difference today to your world!

I. Remember How God has Performed in your Past

Matthew 6:26 "Behold the fowls of the air: for they sow not, neither do they reap, nor gather into barns; yet your heavenly Father feedeth them. Are ye not much better than they?"

II. Remember what God has Promised for your Present

Matthew 6:31-32 "Therefore take no thought, saying, What shall we eat? or, What shall we drink? or, Wherewithal shall we be clothed? [32](For after all these things do the Gentiles seek:) for your heavenly Father knoweth that ye have need of all these things."

III. Remember what God has Planned for your Future

Matthew 6:34 "Take therefore no thought for the morrow: for the morrow shall take thought for the things of itself. Sufficient unto the day is the evil thereof."

IV. Remember what God Requires for Today

Matthew 6:33 "But seek ye first the kingdom of God, and his righteousness; and all these things shall be added unto you."

Worry is useless. Seek the Lord!

I. All Homes Experience Storms

Matthew 7:25 "And the rain descended, and the floods came, and the winds blew, and beat upon that house;"

II. Faulty Homes Erode during Storms

Matthew 7:26-27 "And every one that heareth these sayings of mine, and doeth them not, shall be likened unto a foolish man, which built his house upon the sand: [27]And the rain descended, and the floods came, and the winds blew, and beat upon that house; and it fell: and great was the fall of it. "

III. Faithful Homes Endure Storms

Matthew 7:24-25 "Therefore whosoever heareth these sayings of mine, and doeth them, I will liken him unto a wise man, which built his house upon a rock: [25]And the rain descended, and the floods came, and the winds blew, and beat upon that house; and it fell not: for it was founded upon a rock."

The key to have a faithful home is embracing Scripture

Matthew 7:24 "Therefore whosoever heareth these sayings of mine, and doeth them, I will liken him unto a wise man, which built his house upon a rock:"

Matthew 7:26 "And every one that heareth these sayings of mine, and doeth them not, shall be likened unto a foolish man, which built his house upon the sand:"

I. The Storm on the Sea

Matthew 8:24 "And, behold, there arose a great tempest in the sea, insomuch that the ship was covered with the waves: but he was asleep."

II. The Storm in their Soul

Matthew 8:25 "And his disciples came to him, and awoke him, saying, Lord, save us: we perish."

III. The Sermon in the Ship

Matthew 8:26 "And he saith unto them, Why are ye fearful, O ye of little faith?..."

IV. The Sovereignty of the Savior

Matthew 8:26 "...Then he arose, and rebuked the winds and the sea; and there was a great calm."

V. The Surprise of the Servants

Matthew 8:27 "But the men marvelled, saying, What manner of man is this, that even the winds and the sea obey him!"

I know the Master of the wind!

I. The Prospects

Matthew 9:37 "Then saith he unto his disciples, The harvest truly is plenteous..."

II. The Problem

Matthew 9:37 "...but the laborers are few;"

III. The Plan

Matthew 9:38 "Pray ye therefore the Lord of the harvest, that he will send forth laborers into his harvest."

Let's work His plan to fulfill His purpose!

Matthew 10:42 "And whosoever shall give to drink unto one of these little ones a cup of cold water only in the name of a disciple, verily I say unto you, he shall in no wise lose his reward."

I. The Source of the Gift

"And whosoever..."

II. The Size of the Gift

"And whosoever shall give to drink unto one of these little ones a cup of cold water only..."

III. The Support in the Gift

"And whosoever shall give to drink unto one of these little ones a cup of cold water only **in the name of a disciple...**"

IV. The Security of the Gift

"And whosoever shall give to drink unto one of these little ones a cup of cold water only in the name of a disciple, verily I say unto you, he shall in no wise lose his reward."

Thank God for those who help God's Man!!

I. The Significance of John the Baptist

Matthew 11:11 "Verily I say unto you, Among them that are born of women there hath not risen a greater than John the Baptist . . ."

II. The Superiority of the Saved

Matthew 11:11 "...notwithstanding he that is least in the kingdom of heaven is greater than he."

III. The Severity of Suffering

Matthew 11:12 "And from the days of John the Baptist until now the kingdom of heaven suffereth violence, and the violent take it by force."

No greater news than the fact that God transforms sinners into saints!

I. The Source of the Tongue

Matthew 12:35 "A good man out of the good treasure of the heart bringeth forth good things: and an evil man out of the evil treasure bringeth forth evil things."

II. The Scrutiny of the Tongue

Matthew 12:36 "But I say unto you, That every idle word that men shall speak, they shall give account thereof in the day of judgment."

III. The Seriousness of the Tongue

Matthew 12:37 "For by thy words thou shalt be justified, and by thy words thou shalt be condemned."

Psalms 141:3 "Set a watch, O LORD, before my mouth;
keep the door of my lips."

I. Leave Preadolescence Behind

Matthew 13:54 "And when he was come into his own country, he taught them in their synagogue, insomuch that they were astonished, and said, **Whence hath this man this wisdom...**"

II. Leave Playfulness Behind

Matthew 13:54 "And when he was come into his own country, he taught them in their synagogue, insomuch that they were astonished, and said, Whence hath this man this wisdom, **and these mighty works**?"

III. Leave the Past Behind

Matthew 13:55 "Is not this the carpenter's son? is not his mother called Mary? and his brethren, James, and Joses, and Simon, and Judas?"

IV. Leave Possessions Behind

Matthew 13:56 "And his sisters, are they not all with us? Whence then hath this man all these things?"

V. Leave Provocation Behind

Matthew 13:57 "And they were offended in him. But Jesus said unto them, A prophet is not without honor, save in his own country, and in his own house."

I. Peter began to sink while walking in Obedience and Faith

Matthew 14:28-29 "And Peter answered him and said, Lord, if it be thou, bid me come unto thee on the water. [29]And he said, Come. And when Peter was come down out of the ship, he walked on the water, to go to Jesus."

II. Peter began to sink, when he took his eyes off Jesus

Matthew 14:30 "But when he saw the wind boisterous, he was afraid..."

III. Peter began to sink and the disciples did Nothing

Matthew 14:30 "But when he saw the wind boisterous, he was afraid; and beginning to sink, he cried, saying, Lord, save me."

IV. Peter began to sink and he cried out to the Savior

Matthew 14:30 "But when he saw the wind boisterous, he was afraid; and beginning to sink, he cried, saying, Lord, save me."

V. Peter began to sink and his Savior was near

Matthew 14:31 "And immediately Jesus stretched forth his hand, and caught him..."

VI. Peter began to sink and learned a valuable lesson

Matthew 14:31 "And immediately Jesus stretched forth his hand, and caught him, and said unto him, O thou of little faith, wherefore didst thou doubt?"

Let's keep our eyes on Jesus, and do the impossible!

I. A Religion that Majors on Minors is Messed Up

Matthew 15:1-2 "Then came to Jesus scribes and Pharisees, which were of Jerusalem, saying, [2]Why do thy disciples transgress the tradition of the elders? for they wash not their hands when they eat bread."

II. A Religion that Minimizes the Mandate is Malicious

Matthew 15:3 "But he answered and said unto them, Why do ye also transgress the commandment of God by your tradition?"

III. A Religion that Massages the Messages is Miserable

Matthew 15:4-6 "For God commanded, saying, Honour thy father and mother: and, He that curseth father or mother, let him die the death. [5]But ye say, Whosoever shall say to his father or his mother, It is a gift, by whatsoever thou mightest be profited by me; [6]And honour not his father or his mother, he shall be free. Thus have ye made the commandment of God of none effect by your tradition."

IV. Religion that Misses the Motive is Mean

Matthew 15:7-9 "Ye hypocrites, well did Esaias prophesy of you, saying, [8]This people draweth nigh unto me with their mouth, and honoureth me with their lips; but their heart is far from me. [9]But in vain they do worship me, teaching for doctrines the commandments of men."

Let's honor God by keeping His commandments!!

I. **A Life of Denial**

Matthew 16:24 "Then said Jesus unto his disciples, **If any man will come after me, let him deny himself,** and take up his cross, and follow me."

II. **A Life of Devotion**

Matthew 16:24 "Then said Jesus unto his disciples, **If any man will come after me,** let him deny himself, **and take up his cross,** and follow me."

III. **A Life of Discipleship**

Matthew 16:24 "Then said Jesus unto his disciples, **If any man will come after me,** let him deny himself, and take up his cross, **and follow me.**"

IV. **A Life with Dividends**

Matthew 16:27 "For the Son of man shall come in the glory of his Father with his angels; **and then he shall reward every man according to his works.**"

I. The Sincere Request

Matthew 17:15 "Lord, have mercy on my son: for he is lunatick, and sore vexed: for ofttimes he falleth into the fire, and oft into the water."

II. The Stern Remark

Matthew 17:17 "Then Jesus answered and said, O faithless and perverse generation, how long shall I be with you? how long shall I suffer you? bring him hither to me."

III. The Sensational Restoration

Matthew 17:18 "And Jesus rebuked the devil; and he departed out of him: and the child was cured from that very hour."

IV. The Submissive Remorse

Matthew 17:19 "Then came the disciples to Jesus apart, and said, Why could not we cast him out?"

V. The Successful Remedy

Matthew 17:20-21 "And Jesus said unto them, Because of your un-belief: for verily I say unto you, If ye have faith as a grain of mustard seed, ye shall say unto this mountain, Remove hence to yonder place; and it shall remove; and nothing shall be impossible unto you. [21]Howbeit this kind goeth not out but by prayer and fasting."

Matthew 18:19 "Again I say unto you, That if two of you shall agree on earth as touching any thing that they shall ask, it shall be done for them of my Father which is in heaven."

I. The Partnership in Prayer

"Again I say unto you, That if two of you shall agree on earth..."

II. The Petition in Prayer

"...as touching any thing that they shall ask..."

III. The Promise in Prayer

"...it shall be done for them"

IV. The Provider in Prayer

"...of my Father which is in heaven."

Let us be people who pray!!

I. A Parents Desire of Blessing for their Children

Matthew 19:13 "Then were there brought unto him little children, that he should put his hands on them, and pray: and the disciples rebuked them."

II. A Problem Described of Burdens from their Comrades

Matthew 19:13 "Then were there brought unto him little children, that he should put his hands on them, and pray: and the disciples rebuked them."

III. A Principle Delivered of Benevolence for the Christian

Matthew 19:14-15 "But Jesus said, Suffer little children, and forbid them not, to come unto me: for of such is the kingdom of heaven. [15]And he laid his hands on them, and departed thence."

Let's love, lead, and live godly before our children!

I. The Request from the Sightless

Matthew 20:30 "And, behold, two blind men sitting by the way side, when they heard that Jesus passed by, cried out, saying, Have mercy on us, O Lord, thou Son of David."

II. The Rebuke from Society

Matthew 20:31 "And the multitude rebuked them, because they should hold their peace . . ."

III. The Resolve of the Sinners

Matthew 20:31 "...but they cried the more, saying, Have mercy on us, O Lord, thou Son of David."

IV. The Recognition of the Savior

Matthew 20:32 "And Jesus stood still, and called them, and said, What will ye that I shall do unto you?"

V. The Reliance of the Seeking

Matthew 20:33 "They say unto him, Lord, that our eyes may be opened."

VI. The Reward from the Sovereign

Matthew 20:34 "So Jesus had compassion on them, and touched their eyes: and immediately their eyes received sight, and they followed him."

I can't explain it and I cannot tell you why,
but oh what a difference when Jesus passes by!

Matthew 21:22 "And all things, whatsoever ye shall ask in prayer, believing, ye shall receive."

I. The Restriction of Prayer

"And all things, whatsoever"

II. The Responsibility of Prayer

"ye shall ask in prayer"

III. The Requirement of Prayer

"believing"

IV. The Reward of Prayer

"ye shall receive."

Let's pray and believe great things from God!

Matthew 22:35-36 "Then one of them, which was a lawyer, asked him a question, tempting him, and saying, [36] Master, which is the great commandment in the law?"

I. A Complete Devotion to God

Matthew 22:37-38 "Jesus said unto him, Thou shalt love the Lord thy God with all thy heart, and with all thy soul, and with all thy mind. [38]This is the first and great commandment."

II. A Constant Dedication for Neighbors

Matthew 22:39 "And the second is like unto it, Thou shalt love thy neighbour as thyself."

III. A Condensed Description of the Law

Matthew 22:39 "On these two commandments hang all the law and the prophets."

Let's live out these two simple giant principles today
in the power of the Holy Spirit!

Matthew 23:1 "Then spake Jesus to the multitude, and to his disciples, 2 Saying, The scribes and the Pharisees sit in Moses' seat: 3 All therefore whatsoever they bid you observe, that observe and do; but do not ye after their works: for they say, and do not."

I. Their Words don't match their Works

Matthew 23:3 "...but do not ye after their works: for they say, and do not."

II. Their Requirements don't match their Responsibilities

Matthew 23:4 "For they bind heavy burdens and grievous to be borne, and lay them on men's shoulders; but they themselves will not move them with one of their fingers."

III. Their Attitudes don't match their Actions

Matthew 23:5 "But all their works they do for to be seen of men: they make broad their phylacteries, and enlarge the borders of their garments, 6 And love the uppermost rooms at feasts, and the chief seats in the synagogues,"

IV. Their Titles don't match their Type

Matthew 23:7-10 "And greetings in the markets, and to be called of men, Rabbi, Rabbi. 8 But be not ye called Rabbi: for one is your Master, even Christ; and all ye are brethren. 9 And call no man your father upon the earth: for one is your Father, which is in heaven. 10 Neither be ye called masters: for one is your Master, even Christ."

V. Their Self-Promotions don't match His Self-Denials

Matthew 23:11-12 "But he that is greatest among you shall be your servant. 12 And whosoever shall exalt himself shall be abased; and he that shall humble himself shall be exalted."

I. The Sovereignty of the Father

Matthew 24:36 "But of that day and hour knoweth no man, no, not the angels of heaven, but my Father only.

II. The Sinfulness of Society

Matthew 24:37-38 "But as the days of Noe were, so shall also the coming of the Son of man be. [38]For as in the days that were before the flood they were eating and drinking, marrying and giving in marriage, until the day that Noe entered into the ark,"

III. The Suddenness of His Coming

Matthew 24:39 And knew not until the flood came, and took them all away; so shall also the coming of the Son of man be.

It Could be today. Let's be ready for His soon arrival!

Matthew 25:21 "His lord said unto him, Well done, thou good and faithful servant: thou hast been faithful over a few things, I will make thee ruler over many things: enter thou into the joy of thy lord."

I. Your Performance

"Well done"

II. Your Persistence

"thou good and faithful servant"

III. Your Passion

"servant"

IV. Your Promotion

"I will make thee ruler over many things"

V. Your Prize

"enter thou into the joy of thy lord."

Let's work hard because payday is not far away!

I. The Sacrifice

Matthew 26:7 "There came unto him a woman having an alabaster box of very precious ointment, and poured it on his head, as he sat at meat."

II. The Scorn

Matthew 26:8 "But when his disciples saw it, they had indignation, saying, To what purpose is this waste?"

III. The Sermon

Matthew 26:10 "When Jesus understood it, he said unto them, Why trouble ye the woman? for she hath wrought a good work upon me."

IV. The Significance

Matthew 26:12 "For in that she hath poured this ointment on my body, she did it for my burial."

V. The Statue

Matthew 26:13 "Verily I say unto you, Wheresoever this gospel shall be preached in the whole world, there shall also this, that this woman hath done, be told for a memorial of her."

Thank God for those who sacrifice for the Savior!

I. When Falsely Accused, Jesus was Silent

Matthew 27:12 "And when he was accused of the chief priests and elders, he answered nothing."

II. When Maliciously Accused, Jesus was Silent

Matthew 27:13-14 "Then said Pilate unto him, Hearest thou not how many things they witness against thee? [14]And he answered him to never a word;"

III. When Ridiculously Accused, Jesus was Silent

Matthew 27:14 "And he answered him to never a word; insomuch that the governor marvelled greatly."

It is better to be quiet and people think you're a fool, than to open your mouth and remove all doubt!

I. The Power for World Evangelism

Matthew 28:18 "And Jesus came and spake unto them, saying, All power is given unto me in heaven and in earth."

II. The People for World Evangelism

Matthew 28:19 "Go ye therefore..."

III. The Process for World Evangelism

Matthew 28:19-20 "Go ye therefore, and teach all nations, baptizing them in the name of the Father, and of the Son, and of the Holy Ghost: 20Teaching them to observe all things whatsoever I have commanded you:"

IV. The Promise for World Evangelism

Matthew 28:20 "and, lo, I am with you alway, even unto the end of the world. Amen."

Let's get busy working God's plan!

Mark 1:40 "And there came a leper to him, beseeching him, and kneeling down to him, and saying unto him, If thou wilt, thou canst make me clean."

I. Run to Jesus

"And there came a leper to him"

II. Talk to Jesus

"beseeching him"

III. Submit to Jesus

"and kneeling down to him"

IV. Ask Jesus

"If thou wilt"

V. Believe in Jesus

"thou canst make me clean."

The answer to all of life's problems is Jesus!

I. Compassionate Faith

Mark 2:3 "And they come unto him, bringing one sick of the palsy, which was borne of four."

II. Committed Faith

Mark 2:4 "And when they could not come nigh unto him for the press, they uncovered the roof where he was: and when they had broken it up, they let down the bed wherein the sick of the palsy lay."

IV. Courageous Faith

Mark 2:4 "and when they had broken it up,"

V. Careful Faith

Mark 2:4 "they let down the bed wherein the sick of the palsy lay."

Let's have the faith to get our friends to Jesus!

Mark 3:14 "And he ordained twelve, that they should be with him, and that he might send them forth to preach,"

I. The Call Required of Preachers

"And he ordained twelve,"

II. The Communion Required of Preachers

"that they should be with him,"

III. The Commission Required of Preachers

"and that he might send them forth..."

IV. The Conviction Required of Preachers

"to preach,"

Lord, give us more God-called preachers!

I. A Promise

Mark 4:35 "And the same day, when the even was come, he saith unto them, Let us pass over unto the other side."

II. A Problem

Mark 4:37 "And there arose a great storm of wind, and the waves beat into the ship, so that it was now full."

III. A Preoccupation

Mark 4:38 "And he was in the hinder part of the ship, asleep on a pillow:"

IV. A Panic

Mark 4:38 "and they awake him, and say unto him, Master, carest thou not that we perish?"

V. A Proclamation

Mark 4:39 "And he arose, and rebuked the wind, and said unto the sea, Peace, be still. And the wind ceased, and there was a great calm."

VI. A Precept

Mark 4:40 "And he said unto them, Why are ye so fearful? how is it that ye have no faith?"

VII. A Praise

Mark 4:41 "And they feared exceedingly, and said one to another, What manner of man is this, that even the wind and the sea obey him?"

Storms are no concern when Jesus is in Your boat!

I. Sin's Arrogance

Mark 5:2 "And when he was come out of the ship, immediately there met him out of the tombs a man with an unclean spirit,"

II. Sin's Abode

Mark 5:3 "Who had his dwelling among the tombs;"

III. Sin's Ability

Mark 5:3 "and no man could bind him, no, not with chains:"

IV. Sin's Atrocity

Mark 5:4 "Because that he had been often bound with fetters and chains, and the chains had been plucked asunder by him, and the fetters broken in pieces: neither could any man tame him."

V. Sin's Affliction

Mark 5:5 "And always, night and day, he was in the mountains, and in the tombs, crying, and cutting himself with stones."

VI. Sin's Antidote

Mark 5:6-8 "But when he saw Jesus afar off, he ran and worshipped him, [7]And cried with a loud voice, and said, What have I to do with thee, Jesus, thou Son of the most high God? I adjure thee by God, that thou torment me not. [8]For he said unto him, Come out of the man, thou unclean spirit."

VII. Sin's Abandonment

Mark 5:15 "And they come to Jesus, and see him that was possessed with the devil, and had the legion, sitting, and clothed, and in his right mind: and they were afraid."

Sin's power is no match for the Savior!

Mark 6:50 For they all saw him, and were troubled. And immediately he talked with them, and saith unto them, Be of good cheer: it is I; be not afraid.

I. When Afraid Listen to Jesus

"...And immediately he talked with them,"

II. When Afraid Learn of Jesus

"Be of good cheer:"

III. When Afraid Look to Jesus

"...it is I;"

IV. When Afraid Lean on Jesus

"...be not afraid."

The antidote for fear is faith in Jesus!

I. The Patronization of Legalism

Mark 7:6 "He answered and said unto them, Well hath Esaias prophesied of you hypocrites, as it is written, This people honoureth me with their lips, but their heart is far from me."

II. The Problem of Legalism

Mark 7:7 "Howbeit in vain do they worship me,"

III. The Preaching of Legalism

Mark 7:7 "teaching for doctrines the commandments of men."

IV. The Plan of Legalism

Mark 7:8 "For laying aside the commandment of God, ye hold the tradition of men, as the washing of pots and cups: and many other such like things ye do."

Let our commitment be to God's laws and not man's traditions!

Mark 8:34 "And when he had called the people unto him with his disciples also, he said unto them, Whosoever will come after me, let him deny himself, and take up his cross, and follow me."

I. Devotion to the Savior

"Whosoever will come after me,"

I. Denial of Self

"...let him deny himself"

II. Determination to Submit

"...and take up his cross,"

III. Diligence in Service

"...and follow me."

Lord, let me serve. Lord, let me follow!

I. The Reason You are so Messed up is your Lack of Faith

Mark 9:19 "He answereth him, and saith, O faithless generation, how long shall I be with you? how long shall I suffer you? bring him unto me."

II. The Reason You are so Messed up is your lack of Prayer

Mark 9:29 "And he said unto them, This kind can come forth by nothing, but by prayer and fasting."

III. The Reason You are so Messed up is your lack of Fasting

Mark 9:29 "And he said unto them, This kind can come forth by nothing, but by prayer and fasting."

Jesus is the answer for your messed up life!

I. The Requirements of a Disciple

A. Christ must be First in our priorities

Mark 10:29 "And Jesus answered and said, Verily I say unto you, There is no man that hath left house, or brethren, or sisters, or father, or mother, or wife, or children, or lands,"

B. Christ must be Followed Passionately

Mark 10:29 "for my sake, and the gospel's,"

II. The Rewards of a Disciple

A. The Reward Amount

Mark 10:30 "But he shall receive an hundredfold now in this time, houses, and brethren, and sisters, and mothers, and children, and lands, with persecutions; and in the world to come eternal life."

B. The Reward Date

Mark 10:30 "But he shall receive an hundredfold now in this time, houses, and brethren, and sisters, and mothers, and children, and lands, with persecutions; and in the world to come eternal life."

Truly, serving Jesus is the job of a lifetime!

I. The Mule was Found by God

Mark 11:4 "And they went their way, and found the colt tied by the door without in a place where two ways met;"

II. The Mule was Freed by God

Mark 11:4 "And they went their way, and found the colt tied by the door without in a place where two ways met; and they loose him."

III. The Mule was Famous because of God

Mark 11:7 "And they brought the colt to Jesus, and cast their garments on him; and he sat upon him."

We are worthless sinners;
but when we're found and freed by God, He uses us for His glory!

Mark 12:41 "And Jesus sat over against the treasury, and beheld how the people cast money into the treasury: and many that were rich cast in much."

I. The Description of an Extravagant Giver

Mark 12:42 "And there came a certain poor widow, and she threw in two mites, which make a farthing."

II. The Declaration about Extravagant Giving

Mark 12:43 "And he called unto him his disciples, and saith unto them, Verily I say unto you, That this poor widow hath cast more in, than all they which have cast into the treasury:"

III. The Details of Extravagant Giving

Mark 12:44 "For all they did cast in of their abundance; but she of her want did cast in all that she had, even all her living."

No greater privilege in the world than sacrificing for Jesus!

I. Pretenders

Mark 13:6 "For many shall come in my name, saying, I am Christ; and shall deceive many."

II. Provocations

Mark 13:7 "And when ye shall hear of wars and rumours of wars, be ye not troubled: for such things must needs be; but the end shall not be yet."

III. Plagues

Mark 13:8 "For nation shall rise against nation, and kingdom against kingdom: and there shall be earthquakes in divers places, and there shall be famines and troubles: these are the beginnings of sorrows."

IV. Persecution

Mark 13:9 "But take heed to yourselves: for they shall deliver you up to councils; and in the synagogues ye shall be beaten: and ye shall be brought before rulers and kings for my sake, for a testimony against them."

V. Preaching

Mark 13:10 "And the gospel must first be published among all nations."

> *Keep Your eyes upon the Eastern sky,*
> *lift up your head, redemption draweth nigh!*

I. Serious Sacrifice

Mark 14:3 "And being in Bethany in the house of Simon the leper, as he sat at meat, there came a woman having an alabaster box of ointment of spikenard very precious; and she brake the box, and poured it on his head."

II. Sinful Sarcasm

Mark 14:4-5 "And there were some that had indignation within themselves, and said, Why was this waste of the ointment made? 5For it might have been sold for more than three hundred pence, and have been given to the poor. And they murmured against her."

III. Supernatural Support

Mark 14:6 "And Jesus said, Let her alone; why trouble ye her? she hath wrought a good work on me."

IV. Supreme Significance

Mark 14:7 "For ye have the poor with you always, and whensoever ye will ye may do them good: but me ye have not always."

V. Sincere Service

Mark 14:8 "She hath done what she could: she is come aforehand to anoint my body to the burying."

Let's Do all we can for the Lord!

I. Barabbas Deserved Punishment

Mark 15:7 "And there was one named Barabbas, which lay bound with them that had made insurrection with him, who had committed murder in the insurrection."

II. Jesus Deserved Praise

Mark 15:9-10 "But Pilate answered them, saying, Will ye that I release unto you the King of the Jews? [10]For he knew that the chief priests had delivered him for envy."

III. Jesus Took Punishment so Barabbas could have Praise

Mark 15:12-15 "And Pilate answered and said again unto them, What will ye then that I shall do unto him whom ye call the King of the Jews? [13]And they cried out again, Crucify him.[14]Then Pilate said unto them, Why, what evil hath he done? And they cried out the more exceedingly, Crucify him. [15]And so Pilate, willing to content the people, released Barabbas unto them, and delivered Jesus, when he had scourged him, to be crucified."

The Great Exchange – My sin for His righteousness
2 Corinthians 5:21 "For he hath made him to be sin for us,
who knew no sin; that we might be made the righteousness of God
in him."

I. The Command to the Disciples

Mark 16:15 "And he said unto them, Go ye..."

II. The Commission of the Disciples

Mark 16:15 "And he said unto them, Go ye into all the world, and preach the gospel to every creature."

III. The Confidence of the Disciples

Mark 16:16 "He that believeth and is baptized shall be saved; but he that believeth not shall be damned."

> *You and I are the disciples for this generation.*
> *Let's carry out our Lord's command!*

I. Honor comes from God

Luke 1:28 "And the angel came in unto her, and said, Hail, thou that art highly favoured, the Lord is with thee: blessed art thou among women."

II. Humility pleases God

Luke 1:29 "And when she saw him, she was troubled at his saying, and cast in her mind what manner of salutation this should be."

III. Grace is a gift from God

Luke 1:30 "And the angel said unto her, Fear not, Mary: for thou hast found favour with God."

IV. Callings are bestowed by God

Luke 1:31 "And, behold, thou shalt conceive in thy womb, and bring forth a son, and shalt call his name JESUS."

V. Submissiveness is rewarded by God

Luke 1:38 "And Mary said, Behold the handmaid of the Lord; be it unto me according to thy word. And the angel departed from her."

I thank God, He uses poor peasant boys and girls in His work!

I. Value the Worship of God

Luke 2:41-42 "Now his parents went to Jerusalem every year at the feast of the passover. [42]And when he was twelve years old, they went up to Jerusalem after the custom of the feast."

II. Value the Word of God

Luke 2:43 "And when they had fulfilled the days, as they returned, the child Jesus **tarried behind in Jerusalem;** and Joseph and his mother knew not of it."

III. Value the Ways of God

Luke 2:46 "And it came to pass, that after three days **they found him in the temple,** sitting in the midst of the doctors, both hearing them, and asking them questions."

IV. Value the Work of God

Luke 2:49 "And he said unto them, How is it that ye sought me? wist ye not that I must be about my Father's business?"

V. Value the Will of God

Luke 2:50-51 "And they understood not the saying which he spake unto them. [51]And he went down with them, and came to Nazareth, **and was subject unto them:** but his mother kept all these sayings in her heart."

I. Preaching should include a Salvation Message

Luke 3:3 "And he came into all the country about Jordan, preaching the baptism of repentance for the remission of sins;"

II. Preaching should include a Sanctification Message

Luke 3:4 "As it is written in the book of the words of Esaias the prophet, saying, The voice of one crying in the wilderness, Prepare ye the way of the Lord, **make his paths straight**."

III. Preaching should include a Straight-Forward Message

Luke 3:5-7 "Every valley shall be filled, and every mountain and hill shall be brought low; and the crooked shall be made straight, and the rough ways shall be made smooth; ⁶And all flesh shall see the salvation of God. ⁷Then said he to the multitude that came forth to be baptized of him, O generation of vipers, who hath warned you to flee from the wrath to come?"

IV. Preaching should include a Significant Message

Luke 3:8 "Bring forth therefore fruits worthy of repentance, and begin not to say within yourselves, We have Abraham to our father: for I say unto you, That God is able of these stones to raise up children unto Abraham."

Our world is dying for some old-time preaching of the gospel!

I. Let's Talk about Jesus' Power in Doctrine

Luke 4:31-32 "And came down to Capernaum, a city of Galilee, and taught them on the sabbath days. [32]And **they were astonished at his doctrine:** for his word was with power."

II. Let's Talk about Jesus' Power over Demons

Luke 4:33-35 "And in the synagogue there was a man, which had a spirit of an unclean devil, and cried out with a loud voice, [34]Let us alone; what have we to do with thee, thou Jesus of Nazareth? art thou come to destroy us? I know thee who thou art; the Holy One of God. [35]**And Jesus rebuked him,** saying, Hold thy peace, and come out of him..."

III. Let's Talk about Jesus' Power over Disease

Luke 4:38-39 "And he arose out of the synagogue, and entered into Simon's house. And Simon's wife's mother was taken with a great fever; and they besought him for her. [39]**And he stood over her, and rebuked the fever;** and it left her: and immediately she arose and ministered unto them."

The Old Testament promises Christ.
The New Testament presents Christ.

The Old Testament prophesies Christ.
The New Testament proclaims Christ

The Old Testament symbolizes Christ.
The New Testament sacrifices Christ.

I. The Request from the Savior

Luke 5:4 "Now when he had left speaking, he said unto Simon, Launch out into the deep, and let down your nets for a draught."

II. The Response from the Sailor

Luke 5:5 "And Simon answering said unto him, Master, we have toiled all the night, and have taken nothing: nevertheless at thy word I will let down the net."

A. He Recognized the Savior - "Master"

B. He Recognized the Situation - "we have toiled all the night, and have taken nothing"

C. He Recognized Scripture – "Nevertheless at thy Word"

III. The Reward from the Supplier

Luke 5:6 "And when they had this done, they inclosed a great multitude of fishes: and their net brake."

Submission to the will of God always brings blessings.
Obedience always precedes blessings.

Luke 5:7 "And they beckoned unto their partners, which were in the other ship, that they should come and help them. And they came, and filled both the ships, so that they began to sink."

I. Love Your Adversaries

Luke 6:27 "But I say unto you which hear, Love your enemies . . ."

II. Love Your Avengers

Luke 6:29 "And unto him that smiteth thee on the one cheek offer also the other . . ."

III. Love your Attackers

Luke 6:29 "and him that taketh away thy cloke forbid not to take thy coat also."

IV. Love the Afflicted

Luke 6:30 "Give to every man that asketh of thee . . ."

Loving this way is only possible through Christ!

I. The Resolve of the Sinner

Luke 7:37 "And, behold, a woman in the city, which was a sinner, when she knew that Jesus sat at meat in the Pharisee's house, brought an alabaster box of ointment,"

II. The Repentance of the Sinner

Luke 7:38 "And stood at his feet behind him weeping, and began to wash his feet with tears . . ."

III. The Respect of the Sinner

Luke 7:38 "and did wipe them with the hairs of her head, and kissed his feet, and anointed them with the ointment."

IV. The Righteousness of a Sinner

Luke 7:47 "Wherefore I say unto thee, Her sins, which are many, are forgiven . . ."

Luke 7:48 "And he said unto her, Thy sins are forgiven."

Luke 7:50 "And he said to the woman, Thy faith hath saved thee; go in peace."

Thank God He transforms sinners into saints!

I. **Stolen Seed**

Luke 8:5 "A sower went out to sow his seed: and as he sowed, some fell by the way side; and it was trodden down, and the fowls of the air devoured it."

Luke 8:12 "Those by the way side are they that hear; **then cometh the devil, and taketh away the word** out of their hearts, lest they should believe and be saved."

II. **Shallow Soil**

Luke 8:6 "And some fell upon a rock; and as soon as it was sprung up, it withered away, because it lacked moisture."

Luke 8:13 "They on the rock are they, which, when they hear, receive the word with joy; **and these have no root,** which for a while believe, and in time of temptation fall away."

III. **Strangled Soil**

Luke 8:7 "And some fell among thorns; and the thorns sprang up with it, and choked it."

Luke 8:14 "And that which fell among thorns are they, which, when they have heard, go forth, **and are choked with cares and riches and pleasures of this life,** and bring no fruit to perfection."

III. **Surrendered Soil**

Luke 8:8 "And other fell on good ground, and sprang up, and bare fruit an hundredfold . . ."

Luke 8:15 "But that on the good ground are they, which in an honest and good heart, **having heard the word, keep it, and bring forth fruit** with patience."

I. The Principle of Rest

Luke 9:10 "And the apostles, when they were returned, told him all that they had done. And he took them, **and went aside**"

II. Principle of Priorities

Luke 9:11 "**And the people, when they knew it, followed him: and he received them...**"

III. Principle of Generosity

Luke 9:13 "But he said unto them, Give ye them to eat. And they said, We have no more but five loaves and two fishes; except we should go and buy meat for all this people."

IV. Principle of Organization

Luke 9:14 "For they were about five thousand men. And he said to his disciples, Make them sit down by fifties in a company."

V. Principle of Obedience

Luke 9:15 "And they did so, and made them all sit down."

VI. Principle of Blessing

Luke 9:16 "Then he took the five loaves and the two fishes, and looking up to heaven, **he blessed them,** and brake, and gave to the disciples to set before the multitude.

VII. Principle of Satisfaction

Luke 9:17 "**And they did eat, and were all filled:** and there was taken up of fragments that remained to them twelve baskets."

VIII. Principle of Lordship

Luke 9:18–20 "And it came to pass, as he was alone praying, his disciples were with him: and he asked them, saying, Whom say the people that I am? [19]They answering said, John the Baptist; but some say, Elias; and others say, that one of the old prophets is risen again. [20]He said unto them, But whom say ye that I am? **Peter answering said, The Christ of God.**"

I. A Road of Disaster

Luke 10:30 "And Jesus answering said, **A certain man** went down from Jerusalem to Jericho, **and fell among thieves,** which stripped him of his raiment, and wounded him, and departed, leaving him half dead."

II. A Road of Defilement

Luke 10:31 "And by chance there came down **a certain priest** that way: and when he saw him, **he passed by on the other side.**"

III. A Road of Detainment

Luke 10:32 "And likewise **a Levite,** when he was at the place, came **and looked on him, and passed by on the other side.**"

IV. A Road of Destiny

Luke 10:33 "But a certain Samaritan, as he journeyed, came where he was: **and when he saw him, he had compassion on him,**"

Luke 11:9 "And I say unto you, Ask, and it shall be given you; seek, and ye shall find; knock, and it shall be opened unto you."

I. Promise

"And I say unto you,"

II. Reverence

"Ask,"

III. Diligence

"seek"

IV. Perseverance

"knock"

V. Consequence

"...you, ...you, ...ye, ...you"

When you pray God's way, He provides!

I. The Problem with Greed

Luke 12:13 "And one of the company said unto him, Master, speak to my brother, **that he divide the inheritance with me.**"

II. The Warning Concerning Greed

Luke 12:15 "And he said unto them, Take heed, **and beware of covetousness...**"

III. The Cure for Greed

Luke 12:15 "And he said unto them, Take heed, and beware of covetousness: **for a man's life consisteth not in the abundance of the things which he possesseth**"

A. Remember what you have

Luke 12:16 "And he spake a parable unto them, saying, The ground of a certain rich man **brought forth plentifully:**"

B. Recognize that "THINGS" don't satisfy

Luke 12:17-19 "[17]And he thought within himself, saying, What shall I do, because I have no room where to bestow my fruits? [18]And he said, This will I do: **I will pull down my barns, and build greater;** and there will I bestow all my fruits and my goods. [19]And I will say to my soul, Soul, thou hast much goods laid up for many years; take thine ease, eat, drink, and be merry"

C. Resolve to Combat Greed by Giving

Luke 12:20 "But God said unto him, Thou fool, this night thy soul shall be required of thee: **then whose shall those things be, which thou hast provided?**"

I. The Truth about Atrocities

Luke 13:1-3 "There were present at that season some that told him of the Galileans, **whose blood Pilate had mingled with their sacrifices.** ²And Jesus answering said unto them, Suppose ye that these Galileans were sinners above all the Galileans, because they suffered such things? ³I tell you, Nay: but, except ye repent, ye shall all likewise perish."

Jesus rejected the idea that all tragedy is the result of sin in its victims.

II. The Truth about Accidents

Luke 13:4-5 "Or those eighteen, upon whom the tower in Siloam fell, and slew them, think ye that they were sinners above all men that dwelt in Jerusalem? but, except ye repent, ye shall all likewise perish."

There are accidents in the world because there is sin in the world.

III. The Truth about Repentance

Luke 13:3 "I tell you, Nay: but, **except ye repent, ye shall all likewise perish.**"

THE TRUTH - There are tragedies and accidents in the world today because there is sin in the world. Every person ever born will die in their sin, unless they repent of their sins and accept Christ.

I. Being a Disciple requires Dedication

Luke 14:26 "If any man come to me, and hate not his father, and mother, and wife, and children, and brethren, and sisters, yea, and his own life also, he cannot be my disciple."

II. Being a Disciple requires Determination

Luke 14:27 "And whosoever doth not bear his cross, and come after me, cannot be my disciple."

III. Being a Disciple requires Devotion

Luke 14:33 "So likewise, whosoever he be of you that forsaketh not all that he hath, he cannot be my disciple."

I. **The Rebellion of the Prodigal**

Luke 15:12 "And the younger of them said to his father, **Father, give me** the portion of goods that falleth to me. And he divided unto them his living."

II. **The Ruin of the Prodigal**

Luke 15:13-14 "And not many days after the younger son gathered all together, and took his journey into a far country, and there wasted his substance with riotous living. [14]And when he had spent all, there arose a mighty famine in that land; **and he began to be in want.**"

III. **The Reproach of the Prodigal**

Luke 15:15 "And he went and joined himself to a citizen of that country; **and he sent him into his fields to feed swine.**"

IV. **The Remembrance of the Prodigal**

Luke 15:17-18 "**And when he came to himself,** he said, How many hired servants of my father's have bread enough and to spare, and I perish with hunger! [18]I will arise and go to my father, and will say unto him, Father, I have sinned against heaven, and before thee,"

V. **The Resolve of the Prodigal**

A. He resolved to Return

Luke 15:20 "And he arose, **and came to his father.**"

B. He resolved to Repent

Luke 15:21 "And the son said unto him, **Father, I have sinned** against heaven, and in thy sight, and am no more worthy to be called thy son."

VI. **The Reunion of the Prodigal**

Luke 15:20-24 "And he arose, and came to his father. But when he was yet a great way off, his father saw him, and had compassion, and ran, and fell on his neck, and kissed him. [21]And the son said unto him, Father, I have sinned against heaven, and in thy sight, and am no more worthy to be called thy son. [22]But the father said to his servants, Bring forth the best robe, and put it on him; and put a ring on his hand, and shoes on his feet: [23]And bring hither the fatted calf, and kill it; and let us eat, and be merry: [24]For this my son was dead, and is alive again; he was lost, and is found. And they began to be merry.

I. Be Responsible with What God has Given You (Budget)

Luke 16:1 "And he said also unto his disciples, There was a certain rich man, which had a steward; and the same was accused unto him that **he had wasted his goods.**"

II. Be Resourceful with What God has Given You (Save)

Luke 16:2 "And he called him, and said unto him, How is it that I hear this of thee? **give an account of thy stewardship;** for thou mayest be no longer steward."

III. Be Redistributing What God has Given You (GIVE)

Luke 16:9 "And I say unto you, **Make to yourselves friends of the mammon of unrighteousness;** that, when ye fail, they may receive you into everlasting habitations."

Jesus doesn't want you to just spend your money.
He wants you to invest your money.

Matthew 6:19-21 "Lay not up for yourselves treasures upon earth, where moth and rust doth corrupt, and where thieves break through and steal: [20]But lay up for yourselves treasures in heaven, where neither moth nor rust doth corrupt, and where thieves do not break through nor steal: [21]For where your treasure is, there will your heart be also."

I. The Entreaty for Faith

Luke 17:5 "And the apostles said unto the Lord, Increase our faith."

II. The Example of Faith

Luke 17:6 "And the Lord said, If ye had faith as a grain of mustard seed..."

III. The Encouragement for Faith

Luke 17:6 "And the Lord said, If ye had faith as a grain of mustard seed, ye might say unto this sycamine tree, Be thou plucked up by the root, and be thou planted in the sea; **and it should obey you.**"

The key to great faith is asking a great God for it!!

Luke 18:1 "And he spake a parable unto them to this end, that men ought always to pray, and not to faint;"

I. The People for the Prescription

"...men"

II. The Priority of the Prescription

"...ought"

III. The Persistence of the Prescription

"...always"

III. The Plan of the Prescription

"...to pray"

IV. The Profit from the Prescription

"...and not to faint;"

The remedy for stress is prayer!

Luke 19:5-6 "And when Jesus came to the place, he looked up, and saw him, and said unto him, Zacchaeus, make haste, and come down; for to day I must abide at thy house. ⁶And he made haste, and came down, and received him joyfully."

I. The Sovereignty in the Call

"when Jesus came to the place"

II. The Urgency in the Call

"make haste"

III. The Humility of the Call

"come down"

IV. The Fellowship in the Call

"I must abide at thy house."

V. The Response to the Call

"And he made haste, and came down, and received him joyfully."

Let's be like Zacchaeus, and answer the call!

I. Their Plan of Entrapment

Luke 20:20 "And they watched him, and sent forth spies, which should feign themselves just men, **that they might take hold of his words,** that so they might deliver him unto the power and authority of the governor."

II. Their Praise without Earnestness

Luke 20:21 "And they asked him, saying, Master, we know that thou sayest and teachest rightly, neither acceptest thou the person of any, but teachest the way of God truly:"

III. Their Predicament without Escape

Luke 20:22 "Is it lawful for us to give tribute unto Caesar, or no?"

IV. Their Perversity without Excuse

Luke 20:23 "But he perceived their craftiness, and said unto them, Why tempt ye me?"

V. Their Perplexity without Enthusiasm

Luke 20:24-26 "Shew me a penny. Whose image and superscription hath it? They answered and said, Caesar's. 25And he said unto them, Render therefore unto Caesar the things which be Caesar's, and unto God the things which be God's. 26**And they could not take hold of his words** before the people: **and they marvelled at his answer,**t

The answer for antagonist, is to point them to God!

I. The Means of the Givers - "rich men vs. poor widow"

Luke 21:1-2 "¹And he looked up, and saw the rich men casting their gifts into the treasury. ²And he saw also a certain poor widow casting in thither two mites."

II. The Measurement of the Givers - "gifts vs. two mites"

Luke 21:3 "And he said, Of a truth I say unto you, that this poor widow hath cast in more than they all:"

III. The Message from the Givers - The size of the gift is determined by the faith of the giver

Luke 21:4 "For all these have of their abundance cast in unto the offerings of God: but she of her penury hath cast in all the living that she had."

Little is much when God is in it!

I. Divine Appointments are Conceived By God

Luke 22:8 "And he sent Peter and John, saying, Go and prepare us the passover, that we may eat."

II. Divine Appointments are Constructed By God

Luke 22:10 "And he said unto them, Behold, when ye are entered into the city, there shall a man meet you, bearing a pitcher of water; follow him into the house where he entereth in."

III. Divine Appointments are Coached By God

Luke 22:11 "And ye shall say unto the goodman of the house, The Master saith unto thee, Where is the guestchamber, where I shall eat the passover with my disciples?"

IV. Divine Appointments are Controlled By God

Luke 22:12 "And he shall shew you a large upper room furnished: there make ready."

Be aware of the divine appointments God has for you today!

Luke 23:34 "Then said Jesus, Father, forgive them; for they know not what they do. And they parted his raiment, and cast lots."

I. **Jesus forgave his abusers even though they did not ask for His forgiveness.**

II. **Jesus forgave his abusers while they were abusing Him.**

III. **Jesus forgave his abusers knowing they would continue to abuse Him.**

Jesus forgave because He trusted God with His abuse!

Romans 12:19 "Dearly beloved, avenge not yourselves, but rather give place unto wrath: for it is written, Vengeance is mine; I will repay, saith the Lord."

I. The Purpose of Preaching

Luke 24:27 "And beginning at Moses and all the prophets, he expounded unto them in all the scriptures the things concerning himself."

Expound - to unfold, or to explain

II. The Plan of Preaching

Luke 24:27 "And beginning at Moses and all the prophets, **he expounded unto them in all the scriptures...**"

Every preacher has the responsibility to preach the whole counsel of God.

III. The Point of Preaching

Luke 24:27 "And beginning at Moses and all the prophets, he expounded unto them in all the scriptures **the things concerning himself.**"

The main theme of the Written Word is the Incarnate Word.

Open your Bible anywhere you want and you'll find Jesus.

I. Andrew's Priority

John 1:41 "He **first** findeth his own brother Simon,"

II. Andrew's Persistence

John 1:41 "He first **findeth** his own brother Simon,"

III. Andrew's Passion

John 1:41 "He first findeth **his own brother** Simon,"

IV. Andrew's Plea

John 1:41 "He first findeth his own brother Simon, and saith unto him, **We have found the Messias,** which is, being interpreted, the Christ."

V. Andrew's Purpose

John 1:42 "**And he brought him to Jesus.** And when Jesus beheld him, he said, Thou art Simon the son of Jona: thou shalt be called Cephas, which is by interpretation, A stone."

I. The Command of the Savior

John 2:6 "And there were set there six waterpots of stone, after the manner of the purifying of the Jews, containing two or three firkins apiece. 7Jesus saith unto them, **Fill the waterpots with water.**"

II. The Compliance of the Servants

John 2:7 "Jesus saith unto them, Fill the waterpots with water. **And they filled them up**..."

III. The Care of the Servants

John 2:7 "Jesus saith unto them, Fill the waterpots with water. And they filled them up **to the brim.**"

> *When commanded of the Lord to do something,*
> *let's do it to the best of our ability!*

John 3:16 "For God so loved the world, that he gave his only begotten Son, that whosoever believeth in him should not perish, but have everlasting life.

I. **The People of God's Love**

"For God so loved **the world**"

II. **The Present of God's Love**

"**that he gave his only begotten Son**"

III. **The Plan of God's Love**

"that whosoever **believeth in him**"

IV. **The Provision of God's Love**

"but have everlasting life."

John 4:34 "Jesus saith unto them, My meat is to do the will of him that sent me, and to finish his work."

I. The Necessity of Spiritual Nourishment

"My meat..."

II. The Necessity of Spiritual Obedience

"...is to do the will of him that sent me,"

III. The Necessity of Spiritual Follow Through

"and to finish his work."

Jesus knew and fulfilled His mission.
6What's your mission and how are you fulfilling it.

I. **This Man's Body was Changed when he met Jesus**

John 5:8 "Jesus saith unto him, Rise, **take up thy bed, and walk.**"

II. **This Man's Behavior was Changed when he met Jesus**

John 5:14 "Afterward **Jesus findeth him in the temple,** and said unto him, Behold, thou art made whole: sin no more, lest a worse thing come unto thee."

III. **This Man's Boldness was Changed when he met Jesus**

John 5:15 "The man departed, **and told the Jews that it was Jesus, which had made him whole.**"

I. Storms Come in the Path of Obedience

John 6:16 "And when even was now come, his disciples went down unto the sea,"

II. Storms Make it Appear that God Doesn't Care

John 6:17-19 "¹⁷And entered into a ship, and went over the sea toward Capernaum. And it was now dark, **and Jesus was not come to them.** ¹⁸And the sea arose by reason of a great wind that blew. ¹⁹So when they had rowed about five and twenty or thirty furlongs,"

In the midst of a mighty storm, great darkness and fear, they kept rowing.

III. Storms Reveal Our Weaknesses

John 6:18-19 "And the sea arose by reason of a great wind that blew. ¹⁹So when they had rowed about five and twenty or thirty furlongs, they see Jesus walking on the sea, and drawing nigh unto the ship: **and they were afraid.**"

IV. Storms Should Cause Us to Turn to Jesus

John 6:19-21 "¹⁹...they see Jesus walking on the sea, and drawing nigh unto the ship: and they were afraid. ²⁰But he saith unto them, It is I; be not afraid. ²¹**Then they willingly received him into the ship:** and immediately the ship was at the land whither they went."

V. Storms Pass

John 6:21 "Then they willingly received him into the ship: i"

John 7:28-29 "Then cried Jesus in the temple as he taught, saying, Ye both know me, and ye know whence I am: and I am not come of myself, but he that sent me is true, whom ye know not. [29]But I know him: for I am from him, and he hath sent me."

I. They Knew of the Existence of Christ

"Ye both know me, and ye know whence I am"

II. They Didn't Know of the Equality of Christ!

"and I am not come of myself, he that sent me is true, whom ye know not."

III. They Didn't Know of Epitaph of Christ!

"But I know him: for I am from him, and he hath sent me."

I. **The Existence of Truth**

John 8:32 "And ye shall know the **truth,** and the truth shall make you free."

II. **The Embracement of Truth**

John 8:32 "And **ye shall know the truth,** and the truth shall make you free."

III. **The Exoneration by Truth**

John 8:32 "And ye shall know the truth, and **the truth shall make you free."**

IV. **The Embodiment of Truth**

John 8:36 "If **the Son** therefore shall make you free, ye shall be free indeed."

I. The Condition of lost Sinners

A. Blind - John 9:1"And as Jesus passed by, he saw **a man which was blind** from his birth."

B. Beggar - John 9:8 "The neighbours therefore, and they which before had seen him that he was blind, said, **7**"

II. The Compassion of a Loving Savior

John 9:6-7 "When he had thus spoken, he spat on the ground, and made clay of the spittle, and he anointed the eyes of the blind man with the clay, [7]And said unto him, Go, wash in the pool of Siloam, (which is by interpretation, Sent.) **He went his way therefore, and washed, and came seeing.**"

III. The Celebration of a Living Saint

John 9:38 "And he said, Lord, I believe. **And he worshipped him.**

I. Christ's Possession

John 10:27 "**My sheep** hear my voice, and I know them, and they follow me:"

II. Christ's Present

John 10:28 "And I give unto them eternal life . . ."

Eternal life is a gift. Since you didn't earn it, you can't loose it.

III. Christ's Promise

John 10:28 "And I give unto them eternal life; **and they shall never perish...**"

V. Christ's Power

John 10:28 "And I give unto them eternal life; and they shall never perish, **neither shall any man pluck them out of my hand.**"

VI. Christ's Partner

John 10:29 "My Father, which gave them me, is greater than all; and **no man is able to pluck them out of my Father's hand.**"

You're not holding on to God. He is holding on to you!
Everyone who accepts Christ is placed as a gift in the hands of Christ.
If that wasn't enough, God the Father,
puts his hand over the hands of Jesus!

I. The Personal Responsibility to get a Miracle

John 11:39 "Jesus said, Take ye away the stone..."

II. The Public Rebuke that accompanies a Miracle

John 11:39 "Jesus said, Take ye away the stone. Martha, the sister of him that was dead, saith unto him, **Lord, by this time he stinketh:** for he hath been dead four days."

III. The Profound Requirement to get a Miracle

John 11:40 "Jesus saith unto her, Said I not unto thee, that, **if thou wouldest believe,** thou shouldest see the glory of God?"

God is still in the miracle working business. Do you believe?

I. Martha, a Diligent Worker

John 12:2 "There they made him a supper; **and Martha served:**"

II. Mary, a Devoted Worshiper

John 12:3 "Then took Mary a pound of ointment of spikenard, very costly, **and anointed the feet of Jesus,**"

III. Judas, a Deceiving Wretch

John 12:4-6 "⁴Then saith one of his disciples, Judas Iscariot, Simon's son, which should betray him, ⁵Why was not this ointment sold for three hundred pence, and given to the poor? ⁶This he said, not that he cared for the poor; **but because he was a thief,** and had the bag, and bare what was put therein"

IV. Lazarus, a Delightful Witness

John 12:1-2 "¹Then, six days before the Passover, Jesus came to Bethany, where **Lazarus was who had been dead,** whom He had raised from the dead. ²There they made Him a supper; and Martha served, but Lazarus was one of those who sat at the table with Him."

John 12:11 "because on **account of him many of the Jews went away and believed in Jesus.**"

What would your spiritual portrait look like?

John 13:5 "After that he poureth water into a bason, and began to wash the disciples' feet, and to wipe them with the towel wherewith he was girded."

I. Jesus Served without Exception

He washed all of the disciples' feet

Thomas - The Doubter

James, John, Matthew - Deserters

Peter - The Denier

Judas - The Deceiver

Jesus served them all

II. Jesus Served without Expectation

Jesus washed the feet of all twelve of the disciples, it is not recorded that anyone washed His feet.

III. Jesus Served without Appreciation

It is not recorded that anyone thanked Jesus for washing their feet.

Who and why do you serv?

I. The Promise of Heaven

John 14:1-2 "Let not your heart be troubled: ye believe in God, believe also in me. **²In my Father's house are many mansions: if it were not so, I would have told you**. I go to prepare a place for you."

II. The Particulars of Heaven

A. It is a Specific Place

John 14:2 "In my Father's house...**I go to prepare a place for you.**

B. It is a Spacious Place

John 14:2 "In my Father's house are **many mansions:** if it were not so, I would have told you. I go to prepare a place for you."

C. It is a Special Place

John 14:3 "And if I **go and prepare** a place for you . . ."

D. It is a Spiritual Place

John 14:3 "And if I go and prepare a place for you, I will come again, **and receive you unto myself;** that where I am, there ye may be also."

III. The Permit to Heaven

John 14:4-6 "And whither I go ye know, and the way ye know. ⁵Thomas saith unto him, Lord, we know not whither thou goest; and how can we know the way? **⁶Jesus saith unto him, I am the way,** the truth, and the life: no man cometh unto the Father, but by me."

I. The Joy of the Lord

John 15:11 "These things have I spoken unto you, **that my joy might remain in you,** and that your joy might be full."

II. The Love of the Lord

John 15:12 "This is my commandment, **uu** as I have loved you."

III. Friendship with Lord

John 15:14 "**Ye are my friends,** if ye do whatsoever I command you."

IV. Revelation from the Lord

John 15:15 "Henceforth I call you not servants; for the servant knoweth not what his lord doeth: but I have called you friends; **for all things that I have heard of my Father I have made known unto you.**"

V. Favor with the Lord

John 15:16 "Ye have not chosen me, but **I have chosen you,** and ordained you, that ye should go and bring forth fruit, and that your fruit should remain: **that whatsoever ye shall ask of the Father in my name, he may give it you.**"

I. **The Holy Spirit covicts of the nature of sin**

John 16:8-9 "And when he is come, **he will reprove the world of sin,** and of righteousness, and of judgment: [9] Of sin, because they believe not on me;"

II. **The Holy Spirit convicts of the need of righteousness**

John 16:8 "And when he is come, he will reprove the world of sin, **and of righteousness,** and of judgment:"

Isaiah 64:6a "But we are all as an unclean thing, and all our righteousnesses are as filthy rags;"

III. **The Spirit convicts of the nearness of judgment**

John 16:8 "And when he is come, he will reprove the world of sin, and of righteousness, **and of judgment:**"

I. The Announcement of Christ

John 17:6 "**I have manifested thy name** unto the men which thou gavest me out of the world . . ."

II. The Acceptance of Christ

John 17:6 "I have manifested thy name unto the men which thou gavest me out of the world: thine they were, and thou gavest them me; **and they have kept thy word.**"

III. The Authority of Christ

John 17:8 "For I have given unto them the words which thou gavest me; and they have received them, **and have known surely that I came out from thee, and they have believed** that thou didst send me."

IV. The Assistance of Christ

John 17:9 "**I pray for them:** I pray not for the world, but for them which thou hast given me; for they are thine."

V. The Attributes of Christ

John 17:10 "And **all mine are thine, and thine are mine;** and I am glorified in them."

I. Jesus' Perfection

John 18:29-30 "Pilate then went out unto them, and said, What accusation bring ye against this man? [30] They answered and said unto him, If he were not a malefactor, we would not have delivered him up unto thee."

Hebrews 4:15 "**...but was in all points tempted like as we are, yet without sin.**"

II. Jesus' Prophecy

John 18:31-32 "Then said Pilate unto them, Take ye him, and judge him according to your law. The Jews therefore said unto him, It is not lawful for us to put any man to death. [32]**That the saying of Jesus might be fulfilled,** which he spake, signifying what death he should die."

III. Jesus' Purpose

John 18:37 "Pilate therefore said unto him, Art thou a king then? Jesus answered, Thou sayest that I am a king. **To this end was I born, and for this cause came I into the world, that I should bear witness unto the truth.** Every one that is of the truth heareth my voice."

IV. Jesus' Purpose

John 18:37 "Pilate therefore said unto him, Art thou a king then? Jesus answered, Thou sayest that I am a king. To this end was I born, and for this cause came I into the world, that I should bear witness unto the truth. **Every one that is of the truth heareth my voice.**"

I. A Statement of Compassion

John 19:25-27 "Now there stood by the cross of Jesus his mother, and his mother's sister, Mary the wife of Cleophas, and Mary Magdalene. 26When Jesus therefore saw his mother, and the disciple standing by, whom he loved, he saith unto his mother, Woman, behold thy son! 27Then saith he to the disciple, Behold thy mother! And from that hour that disciple took her unto his own home"

II. A Statement of Calamity

John 19:28 "After this, Jesus knowing that all things were now accomplished, that the scripture might be fulfilled, saith, I thirst."

III. A Statement of Conquest

John 19:30 "When Jesus therefore had received the vinegar, he said, It is finished: and he bowed his head, and gave up the ghost."

I. Her Sorrow caused her to Miss Jesus

John 20:11 "But Mary stood without at the sepulchre **weeping:** and as she wept, she stooped down, and looked into the sepulchre,"

When Sorrow is Uncontrolled We Focus on the Wrong Things

II. Her Situation caused her to miss Jesus

John 20:12-13 "**And seeth two angels in white sitting,** the one at the head, and the other at the feet, where the body of Jesus had lain.[13]And they say unto her, Woman, why weepest thou? She saith unto them, Because they have taken away my Lord, and I know not where they have laid him."

Our outlook grows dark when we are too focused on people instead of God.

III. Her Short Sightedness caused her to miss Jesus

John 20:14-15 "And when she had thus said, she turned herself back, **and saw Jesus standing, and knew not that it was Jesus.** [15]Jesus saith unto her, Woman, why weepest thou? whom seekest thou? She, supposing him to be the gardener, saith unto him, Sir, if thou have borne him hence, tell me where thou hast laid him, and I will take him away."

Mary was looking for a corpse instead of the living Lord.

IV. Her Standpoint caused her to miss Jesus

John 20:16 "Jesus saith unto her, Mary. **She turned herself,** and saith unto him, Rabboni; which is to say, Master."

Many times during the tragedies of life we miss Jesus
because we're going in the wrong direction.

I. The Principle of Waiting

John 21:2 "There were together Simon Peter, and Thomas called Didymus, and Nathanael of Cana in Galilee, and the sons of Zebedee, and two other of his disciples."

II. The Principle of Fruitlessness

John 21:3 "Simon Peter saith unto them, I go a fishing. They say unto him, We also go with thee. They went forth, and entered into a ship immediately; **and that night they caught nothing.**"

III. The Principle of Obedience

John 21:6 "And he said unto them, Cast the net on the right side of the ship, and ye shall find. **They cast therefore,** and now they were not able to draw it for the multitude of fishes."

IV. The Principle of Abundance

John 21:6 "And he said unto them, Cast the net on the right side of the ship, and ye shall find. They cast therefore, **and now they were not able to draw it for the multitude of fishes.**"

V. The Principle of Tenderness

John 21:7 "**Therefore that disciple whom Jesus loved** saith unto Peter, It is the Lord."

VI. The Principle of Devotion

John 21:7 "Therefore that disciple whom Jesus loved saith unto Peter, It is the Lord. Now **when Simon Peter heard that it was the Lord,** he girt his fisher's coat unto him, (for he was naked,) **and did cast himself into the sea.**"

VII. The Principle of Provision

John 21:9 "As soon then as they were come to land, **they saw a fire of coals there, and fish laid thereon, and bread.**"

VIII. The Principle of Co-Laboring

John 21:10 "Jesus saith unto them, **Bring of the fish which ye have now caught.**"

IX. The Principle of Communion/Fellowship

John 21:12 "Jesus saith unto them, I And none of the disciples durst ask him, Who art thou? knowing that it was the Lord."

I. **The Presence of the Savior Changed Them**

Acts 1:3 "To whom also **he shewed himself alive** after his passion by many infallible proofs, being seen of them forty days . . ."

II. **The Preaching of the Savior Changed Them**

Acts 1:3 "To whom also he shewed himself alive after his passion by many infallible proofs, being seen of them forty days, and **speaking of the things pertaining to the kingdom of God:"**

III. **The Promise of the Savior Changed Them**

Acts 1:4 "And, being assembled together with them, commanded them that they should not depart from Jerusalem, but **wait for the promise of the Father,** which, saith he, ye have heard of me."

IV. **The Plan of the Savior Changed Them**

Acts 1:8 "But ye shall receive power, after that the Holy Ghost is come upon you: and ye shall be witnesses unto me both in Jerusalem, and in all Judaea, and in Samaria, and unto the uttermost part of the earth."

V. **The Parting of the Savior Changed Them**

Acts 1:9-11 "And when he had spoken these things, while they beheld, he was taken up; and a cloud received him out of their sight. [10] And while they looked stedfastly toward heaven as he went up, behold, two men stood by them in white apparel; [11] Which also said, Ye men of Galilee, why stand ye gazing up into heaven? this same Jesus, which is taken up from you into heaven, shall so come in like manner as ye have seen him go into heaven."

VI. **The Prayer's to the Savior Changed Them**

Acts 1:14 "These all continued with one accord in prayer and supplication..."

VII. **The Preaching about the Savior Changed Them**

Acts 1:15-16 "And in those days Peter stood up in the midst of the disciples, and said, (the number of names together were about an hundred and twenty,) [16]Men and brethren, this scripture must needs have been fulfilled, which the Holy Ghost by the mouth of David spake before concerning Judas, which was guide to them that took Jesus."

I. **They were a Saved Church**

Acts 2:41 "...and the same day there were added unto them about three thousand souls."

II. **They were a Spiritual Church**

Acts 2:42 "...continued stedfastly"

III. **They were a Social Church**

Acts 2:42 "...and fellowship, and in breaking of bread,"

IV. **They were a Sincere Church**

Acts 2:42 "...and in prayers."

V. **They were a Sanctified Church**

Acts 2:43 "And fear came upon every soul:"

VI. **They were a Supernatural Church**

Acts 2:43 "and many wonders and signs were done by the apostles."

VII. **They were a Sacrificial Church**

Acts 2:44-45 "44And all that believed were together, and had all things common; 45And sold their possessions and goods, and parted them to all men, as every man had need."

VIII. **They were a Sold Out Church**

Acts 2:46 "continuing daily...and singleness of heart,"

IX. **They were a Singing Church**

Acts 2:47 "Praising God . . ."

X. **They were a Successful Church**

Acts 2:47 "And the Lord added to the church daily such as should be saved."

I. A Pitiful Man

Acts 3:2 "...lame from his mother's womb"

II. A Powerful Miracle

Acts 3:4-6 "And Peter, fastening his eyes upon him with John, said, Look on us. ⁵And he gave heed unto them, expecting to receive something of them. ⁶Then Peter said, Silver and gold have I none; but such as I have give I thee: **In the name of Jesus Christ of Nazareth rise up and walk.**"

III. A Puzzled Multitude

Acts 3:9-11 "...the lame man which was healed held Peter and John,...**greatly wondering.**"

IV. The Pointed Message

Acts 3:12 "And when Peter saw it, he answered unto the people, Ye men of Israel, **why marvel ye at this?** or why look ye so earnestly on us, as though by our own power or holiness we had made this man to walk?"

A. What God Did

Acts 3:15 "And killed the Prince of life, whom God hath raised from the dead; whereof we are witnesses."

B. What God is Going to Do

Acts 3:20-21 "And he shall send Jesus Christ,"

C. Why God Did It

Acts 3:26 "...sent him to bless you, in turning away every one of you from his iniquities."

Six Steps to Respond Properly to Persecution when it Comes

I. Be Spirit Filled

Acts 4:8 "Then Peter, filled with the Holy Ghost, said unto them..."

II. Be Submissive

Acts 4:8 "Then Peter, filled with the Holy Ghost, said unto them, **Ye rulers of the people, and elders of Israel,**"

III. Be Secure

Acts 4:9-10 "If we this day be examined of the good deed done to the impotent man, by what means he is made whole; [10]Be it known unto you all, and to all the people of Israel, that by the name of Jesus Christ of Nazareth, whom ye crucified, whom God raised from the dead, even by him doth this man stand here before you whole."

IV. Be Surrendered

Acts 4:17-19 "But that it spread no further among the people, let us straitly threaten them, that they speak henceforth to no man in this name. [18]And they called them, and commanded them not to speak at all nor teach in the name of Jesus. [19]But Peter and John answered and said unto them, Whether it be right in the sight of God to hearken unto you more than unto God, judge ye."

V. Be Supported

Acts 4:23 "And being let go, they went to their own company, and reported all that the chief priests and elders had said unto them."

VI. Be Stedfast

Acts 4:29 "And now, Lord, behold their threatenings: and grant unto thy servants, that with all boldness they may speak thy word,

I. A Satanic Plot

Acts 5:1 "¹But a certain man named Ananias, with Sapphira his wife, sold a possession, **²And kept back part of the price,** his wife also being privy to it, and brought a certain part, and laid it at the apostles' feet."

Why would they do this Wicked Deed? Three Reasons

A. They had No Contentment with their Stuff

B. They had No Control over Self

C. They had No Consideration for the Savior

II. A Severe Punishment

Acts 5:3-6 "But Peter said, Ananias, why hath Satan filled thine heart to lie to the Holy Ghost, and to keep back part of the price of the land? ⁴Whiles it remained, was it not thine own? and after it was sold, was it not in thine own power? why hast thou conceived this thing in thine heart? **thou hast not lied unto men, but unto God.** ⁵And Ananias hearing these words fell down, and gave up the ghost: and great fear came on all them that heard these things. ⁶And the young men arose, wound him up, and carried him out, and buried him."

III. A Supernatural Power

Acts 5:12 "And by the hands of the apostles were many signs and wonders wrought among the people; (and they were all with one accord in Solomon's porch."

I. The Reason for Deacons

A. The Concern for the Widows

Acts 6:1 "And in those days, when the number of the disciples was multiplied, there arose a murmuring of the Grecians against the Hebrews, **because their widows were neglected** in the daily ministration."

B. The Commitment of the Apostles

Acts 6:2, 4 "²Then the twelve called the multitude of the disciples unto them, and said, **It is not reason that we should leave the word** of God, and serve tables. ⁴But we will give ourselves continually to prayer, and to the ministry of the word."

II. The Requirements of Deacons

Acts 6:3 "Wherefore, brethren, look ye out among you seven men of honest report, full of the Holy Ghost and wisdom, whom we may appoint over this business."

III. The Results of Deacons

A. Word of God Increased

Acts 6:7 "**And the word of God increased...**"

B. The Church Grew

Acts 6:7 "And the word of God increased; **and the number of the disciples multiplied in Jerusalem greatly...**"

C. People were Saved

Acts 6:7 "And the word of God increased; and the number of the disciples multiplied in Jerusalem greatly; **and a great company of the priests were obedient to the faith.**"

I. The Character of Stephen

A. He was full of Faith.

Acts 6:5 "And the saying pleased the whole multitude: and they chose Stephen, **a man full of faith...**"

B. He was full of the Holy Spirit.

Acts 6:5 "And the saying pleased the whole multitude: and they chose Stephen, a man full of faith **and of the Holy Ghost...**"

C. He was full of power.

Acts 6:8 "And Stephen, full of faith **and power,** did great wonders and miracles among the people."

II. The Conflict of Stephen

Acts 6:9 "Then there arose certain of the synagogue, which is called the synagogue of the Libertines, and Cyrenians, and Alexandrians, and of them of Cilicia and of Asia, **disputing with Stephen.**"

III. The Condemnation of Stephen

Acts 7:54 "When they heard these things, they were cut to the heart, and **they gnashed on him with their teeth.**"

IV. The Coronation of Stephen

Acts 7:60 "And he kneeled down, and cried with a loud voice, Lord, lay not this sin to their charge. And when he had said this, **he fell asleep.**"

I. The Sorrow of the Church

Acts 8:2 "And devout men carried Stephen to his burial, **and made great lamentation over him.**"

II. The Suffering of the Church

Acts 8:3 "As for Saul, **he made havock of the church,** entering into every house, and haling men and women committed them to prison."

III. The Saturation of the Church

Acts 8:4 "Therefore they that were scattered abroad **went every where preaching the word.**"

Acts 9:31 "Then had the churches rest throughout all Judaea and Galilee and Samaria, and were edified; and walking in the fear of the Lord, and in the comfort of the Holy Ghost, were multiplied."

I. Edification of the Saints

"and were edified;"

II. Sanctification of the Saints

"and walking in the fear of the Lord,"

III. Multiplication of the Saints

"...were multiplied."

I. The Peace of God's Son

Acts 10:36 "The word which God sent unto the children of Israel, **preaching peace by Jesus Christ:** (he is Lord of all:)"

II. The Position of God's Son

Acts 10:36 "The word which God sent unto the children of Israel, preaching peace by Jesus Christ: **(he is Lord of all:)**"

III. The Pronouncement of God's Son

Acts 10:37 "That word, I say, ye know, **which was published throughout all Judaea,** and began from Galilee, after the baptism which John preached;"

IV. The Power of God's Son

Acts 10:38 "How God anointed Jesus of Nazareth **with the Holy Ghost and with power:** who went about doing good, and healing all that were oppressed of the devil; for God was with him."

V. The Product of God's Son

Acts 10:38 "How God anointed Jesus of Nazareth with the Holy Ghost and with power: **who went about doing good, and healing all that were oppressed of the devil;** for God was with him."

VI. The Presence of God's Son

Acts 10:38 "How God anointed Jesus of Nazareth with the Holy Ghost and with power: who went about doing good, and healing all that were oppressed of the devil; **for God was with him.**"

I. This Church was a Persecuted Church

Acts 11:19 "Now they which were scattered abroad **upon the persecution that arose** about Stephen travelled as far as Phenice, and Cyprus, and Antioch,"

II. This Church was a Friendly Church

Acts 11:20 "And some of them were men of Cyprus and Cyrene, which, when they were come to Antioch, **spake unto the Grecians...**"

III. This Church was a Witnessing Church

Acts 11:20 "And some of them were men of Cyprus and Cyrene, which, when they were come to Antioch, spake unto the Grecians, **preaching the LORD Jesus.**"

IV. This Church was a Grace-Filled Church

Acts 11:22-23 "²²Then tidings of these things came unto the ears of the church which was in Jerusalem: and they sent forth Barnabas, that he should go as far as Antioch. ²³Who, when he came, **and had seen the grace of God, was glad,** and exhorted them all, that with purpose of heart they would cleave unto the Lord."

V. This Church was a Diligent Church

Acts 11:26 "And when he had found him, he brought him unto Antioch. And it came to pass, that a whole year they assembled themselves with the church, and taught much people. **And the disciples were called Christians first in Antioch.**"

Acts 12:5 "Peter therefore was kept in prison: but prayer was made without ceasing of the church unto God for him."

I. Committed Prayer

"but prayer was made..."

II. Continual Prayer

"without ceasing..."

III. Corporate Prayer

"of the church"

IV. Concerted Prayer

"unto God"

V. Concentrated Prayer

"for him."

Acts 13:2-3 "²As they ministered to the Lord, and fasted, the Holy Ghost said, Separate me Barnabas and Saul for the work whereunto I have called them. ³And when they had fasted and prayed, and laid their hands on them, they sent them away."

I. The Prerequisite of a Call - Service

"As they ministered to the Lord,"

II. The Purity of a Call - Sincerity

"and fasted,"

III. The Priority of a Call -Separation

"Separate me Barnabas and Saul for the work"

IV. The Person of the Call -Savior

"I have called them."

V. The Partners in the Call - Saints

"And when **they** had fasted and prayed, and laid **their** hands on **them, they** sent **them** away."

Acts 14:19-20 "[19]And there came thither certain Jews from Antioch and Iconium, who persuaded the people, and, having stoned Paul, drew him out of the city, supposing he had been dead. [20]Howbeit, as the disciples stood round about him, he rose up, and came into the city: and the next day he departed with Barnabas to Derbe."

I. Be Surrounded by Believers

"as the disciples stood round about him,"

II. Be Steadfast in Returning to the Battle

"he rose up,"

III. Be Sold Out in Serving Jesus

"and came into the city:"

IV. Be Supported by Friends

"and the next day he departed with Barnabas"

V. Be Sure to Follow God's Plan

"to Derbe."

I. Exhorters

Acts 15:32 "And Judas and Silas, being prophets also themselves, **exhorted the brethren** with many words, and confirmed them."

II. Extensive

Acts 15:32 "And Judas and Silas, being prophets also themselves, exhorted the brethren **with many words,** and confirmed them."

III. Encouragers

Acts 15:32 "And Judas and Silas, being prophets also themselves, exhorted the brethren with many words, and **confirmed them.**"

IV. Exployers

Acts 15:33 "And **after they had tarried there a space, they were let go** in peace from the brethren unto the apostles."

I. **Jail Houses Turn into Churches when Christ is Entreated**

Acts16:25 "And at midnight **Paul and Silas prayed...**"

II. **Jail Houses Turn into Churches when the Creator is Exalted**

Acts 16:25 "And at midnight Paul and Silas prayed, and **sang praises unto God:** and the prisoners heard them."

I Thessalonians 5:18 "In every thing give thanks: for this is the will of God in Christ Jesus concerning you."

III. **Jail Houses Turn into Churches when Courage is Exhibited**

Acts 16:25 "And at midnight Paul and Silas prayed, and sang praises unto God: **and the prisoners heard them.**"

IV. **Jail Houses Turn into Churches when Character is Evidenced**

Acts 16:26-28 "And suddenly there was a great earthquake, so that the foundations of the prison were shaken: and immediately all the doors were opened, and every one's bands were loosed. [27] And the keeper of the prison awaking out of his sleep, and seeing the prison doors open, he drew out his sword, and would have killed himself, supposing that the prisoners had been fled. [28] But Paul cried with a loud voice, saying, Do thyself no harm: for **we are all here.**"

They stuck around...WHY? They knew souls were at stake.

They knew their testimony was at stake."

I. Jesus is Lord

Acts 17:22-25, "Then Paul stood in the midst of Mars' hill, and said, Ye men of Athens, I perceive that in all things ye are too superstitious. [23]For as I passed by, and beheld your devotions, I found an altar with this inscription, TO THE UNKNOWN GOD. Whom therefore ye ignorantly worship, him declare I unto you. [24]God that made the world and all things therein, seeing **that he is Lord of heaven and earth,** dwelleth not in temples made with hands; [25]Neither is worshipped with men's hands, as though he needed any thing, seeing he giveth to all life, and breath, and all things;"

II. Jesus is Lord Alone

Acts 17:26 "And hath made of one blood all nations of men for to dwell on all the face of the earth, and hath determined the times before appointed, and the bounds of their habitation;"

Acts 17:28, **For in him** we live, and move, and have our being; (We Exist)

III. Jesus is Lord of All People

Acts 17:30 "And the times of this ignorance God winked at; but now commandeth **all men every where** to repent."

IV. Jesus is Lord of All Time

Acts 17:31 "Because he hath appointed a day, in the which **he will judge the world in righteousness** by that man whom he hath ordained; whereof he hath given assurance unto all men, in that he hath raised him from the dead."

Acts 18:9-10 "Then spake the Lord to Paul in the night by a vision, Be not afraid, but speak, and hold not thy peace: 10 For I am with thee, and no man shall set on thee to hurt thee: for I have much people in this city."

I. Confidence

"Be not Afraid"

II. Communicate

"but speak"

III. Companion

"For I am with thee"

IV. Courage

"and no man shall set on thee to hurt thee"

V. Comrades

"for I have much people in this city."

I. **The Proof of a Disciple – The Indwelling of the Spirit**

Acts 19:2 "He said unto them, Have ye received **the Holy Ghost** since ye believed? And they said unto him, We have not so much as heard whether there be any Holy Ghost."

II. **The Puzzlement of these Disciple – Ignorance of the Spirit**

Acts 19:2 "He said unto them, Have ye received the Holy Ghost since ye believed? And they said unto him, **We have not so much as heard whether there be any Holy Ghost.**"

III. **The Problem of these Disciple – Living under the Law**

Acts 19:3 "And he said unto them, Unto what then were ye baptized? And they said, **Unto John's baptism.**"

IV. **The Power of these Disciples**

Acts 19:5-6 "[5]When they heard this, they were baptized in the name of the Lord Jesus. [6]And when Paul had laid his hands upon them, **the Holy Ghost came on them;** and they spake with tongues, and prophesied."

I. Take Heed to Yourself

Acts 20:28 "**Take heed therefore unto yourselves,** and to all the flock, over the which the Holy Ghost hath made you overseers, to feed the church of God, which he hath purchased with his own blood."

The pastor's character matters as well as his beliefs.

II. Take Heed to Flock

Acts 20:28 "Take heed therefore unto yourselves, and to all the flock, over the which the Holy Ghost hath made you overseers, to feed the church of God, which he hath purchased with his own blood."

A. The pastor's assignment-all the flock

B. The pastor's appointment-Holy Ghost hath made you overseers,

C. The pastor's activity-feed the church

The job of the pastor is not to entertain the flock but to feed the flock!

I. **The Reception of Missionaries**

Acts 21:17 "And when we were come to Jerusalem, **the brethren received us gladly**."

II. **The Reporting of Missionaries**

Acts 21:18-19 "[18]And the day following Paul went in with us unto James; and all the elders were present. [19]And when he had saluted them, **he declared particularly what things God had wrought among the Gentiles by his ministry**."

III. **The Rejoicing with Missionaries**

Acts 21:20 "**And when they heard it, they glorified the Lord,** and said unto him, Thou seest, brother, how many thousands of Jews there are which believe; and they are all zealous of the law:"

I. The Requirement for Discipleship - Salvation

Acts 22:10 "And I said, **What shall I do, Lord?** And the Lord said unto me, Arise, and go into Damascus; and there it shall be told thee of all things which are appointed for thee to do."

II. The Reputation of a Discipler - Sincerity

Acts 22:12 "And one **Ananias, a devout man** according to the law, having a good report of all the Jews which dwelt there,"

III. The Resources of a Discipler – The Spirit

Acts 22:13 "Came unto me, and stood, and said unto me, **Brother Saul, receive thy sight.** And the same hour I looked up upon him."

IV. The Recognition of a Discipler – The Savior

Acts 22:14 "And he said, The **God of our fathers hath chosen thee,** that thou shouldest know his will, and see that Just One, and shouldest hear the voice of his mouth."

V. The Reason for Discipleship – Support

Acts 22:15 "**For thou shalt be his witness unto all men** of what thou hast seen and heard."

VI. The Resolve of Discipleship – Swiftness

Acts 22:16 "**And now why tarriest thou?** arise, and be baptized, and wash away thy sins, calling on the name of the Lord."

Acts 23:1 "And Paul, earnestly beholding the council, said, Men and brethren, I have lived in all good conscience before God until this day."

I. **Be Sincere**

"earnestly"

II. **Be Sweet**

"Men and brethren"

III. **Be Straight**

"good conscience"

IV. **Be Spiritual**

"before God"

V. **Be Stedfast**

"until this day"

Acts 24:16 "And herein do I exercise myself, to have always a conscience void of offence toward God, and toward men."

I. A Clear Conscience requires Commitment

"exercise myself"

II. A Clear Conscience requires Consistency

"always"

III. A Clear Conscience requires Consecration

"void of offence"

IV. A Clear Conscience requires Constancy

"toward God, and toward men."

Acts 25:7-8 "⁷And when he was come, the Jews which came down from Jerusalem stood round about, and laid many and grievous complaints against Paul, which they could not prove. ⁸While he answered for himself, Neither against the law of the Jews, neither against the temple, nor yet against Caesar, have I offended any thing at all."

I. The Accusers

"stood round about"

II. The Accusations

"laid many grievous complaints"

III. The Allegations

"which they could not prove."

IV. The Authenticity

"he answered for himself, Neither against the law of the Jews, neither against the temple, nor yet against Caesar, have I offended any thing at all."

Acts 26:16-18 "But rise, and stand upon thy feet: for I have appeared unto thee for this purpose, to make thee a minister and a witness both of these things which thou hast seen, and of those things in the which I will appear unto thee; [17]Delivering thee from the people, and from the Gentiles, unto whom now I send thee, [18]To open their eyes, and to turn them from darkness to light, and from the power of Satan unto God, that they may receive forgiveness of sins, and inheritance among them which are sanctified by faith that is in me."

I. Shine the Light of the Savior

"To open their eyes, and to turn them from darkness to light"

II. Show the Lord and his Strength

"and from the power of Satan unto God,"

III. Share the News of Salvation

"that they may receive forgiveness of sins"

IV. Stress the Inheritance of the Sanctified

"and inheritance among them which are sanctified by faith that is in me."

I. **The Suddenness of the Storm**

Acts 27:14 "But not long after there arose..."

II. **The Strength of the Storm**

Acts 27:14 "...a tempestuous wind, called Euroclydon."

III. **The Shaking of the Ship**

Acts 27:15 "And when the ship was caught, and could not bear up into the wind, we let her drive."

IV. **The Struggle of the Sailors**

Acts 27:16 "And running under a certain island which is called Clauda, we had much work to come by the boat:"

V. **The Surrender of their Stuff**

Acts 27:18 "And we being exceedingly tossed with a tempest, the next day they lightened the ship;"

VI. **The Service of the Seafarers**

Acts 27:19 "And the third day we cast out with our own hands the tackling of the ship."

VII. **The Submission of their Strategy**

Acts 27:20 "And when neither sun nor stars in many days appeared, and no small tempest lay on us, all hope that we should be saved was then taken away.

VIII. **The Sermon from the Slave**

Acts 27:21-24 "But after long abstinence Paul stood forth in the midst of them, and said, Sirs, ye should have hearkened unto me, and not have loosed from Crete, and to have gained this harm and loss. [22]And now I exhort you to be of good cheer: for there shall be no loss of any man's life among you, but of the ship. [23]For there stood by me this night the angel of God, whose I am, and whom I serve, [24]Saying, Fear not, Paul; thou must be brought before Caesar: and, lo, God hath given thee all them that sail with thee."

Acts 28:1-2 "And when they were escaped, then they knew that the island was called Melita. ²And the barbarous people shewed us no little kindness: for they kindled a fire, and received us every one, because of the present rain, and because of the cold."

I. What Society Believed

"barbarous people"

II. What the Seamen Beheld

"no little kindness"

A. Cared for them Physically

"for they kindled a fire"

B. Cared for them Emotionally

"and received us every one"

III. What Scripture Brings Out

Acts 28:4-6 "And when the barbarians saw the venomous beast hang on his hand, they said among themselves, No doubt this man is a murderer, whom, though he hath escaped the sea, yet vengeance suffereth not to live. ⁵ And he shook off the beast into the fire, and felt no harm. ⁶ Howbeit they looked when he should have swollen, or fallen down dead suddenly: but after they had looked a great while, and saw no harm come to him, they changed their minds, and said that he was a god."

Acts 10:34 "Then Peter opened his mouth, and said, Of a truth I perceive that God is no respecter of persons:"

Romans 1:16 "For I am not ashamed of the gospel of Christ: for it is the power of God unto salvation to every one that believeth; to the Jew first, and also to the Greek."

I. Praise of the Gospel

"I am not ashamed"

II. Person of the Gospel

"the gospel of Christ"

III. Power of the Gospel

"it is the power of God"

IV. Purpose of the Gospel

"unto salvation"

V. People of the Gospel

"to everyone that believeth"

VI. Prerequisite of the Gospel

"believeth"

Romans 2:6 "Who will render to every man according to his deeds:"

I. The Judge

"Who" - Jesus

II. The Judgment

"render"

III. The Judged

"every man"

IV. The Justice

"according to his deeds"

Are you ready to meet your Judge?

Romans 3:22 "Even the righteousness of God which is by faith of Jesus Christ unto all and upon all them that believe: for there is no difference:"

I. The Prerequisite for Heaven

"the righteousness of God "

II. The Pathway to Heaven

"which is by faith of Jesus Christ"

III. The People of Heaven

"unto all and upon all them that believe:"

I. The Challenge of Faith

Romans 4:18 "Who against hope believed in hope"

II. The Courage of Faith

Romans 4:19 "And being not weak in faith"

III. The Conflict of Faith

Romans 4:20 "He staggered not at the promise of God through unbelief;"

IV. The Commitment of Faith

Romans 4:20 "but was strong in faith, giving glory to God;"

V. The Confidence of Faith

Romans 4:21 "And being fully persuaded that, what he had promised, he was able also to perform."

VI. The Compensation of Faith

Romans 4:22 "And therefore it was imputed to him for righteousness."

I. Peace with God

Romans 5:1 "Therefore being justified by faith, **we have peace with God** through our Lord Jesus Christ"

II. Fellowship with God

Romans 5:2 "By whom also **we have access by faith** into this grace wherein we stand"

III. Praise to God

Romans 5:2 "and rejoice in hope of the glory of God."

IV. Suffering for God

Romans 5:3-4 "[3]And not only so, but **we glory in tribulations** also: knowing that tribulation worketh patience; [4]And patience, experience; and experience, hope:"

V. Boldness for God

Romans 5:5 "And **hope maketh not ashamed;** because the love of God is shed abroad in our hearts by the Holy Ghost which is given unto us."

The Christian life is a wonderful life!

I. Recognize the Truth

Romans 6:11 "Likewise **reckon ye also yourselves to be dead indeed unto sin,** but alive unto God through Jesus Christ our Lord."

II. Reject Evil

Romans 6:12 "**Let not sin therefore reign in your mortal body,** that ye should obey it in the lusts thereof."

III. Resist Temptation

Romans 6:13 "Neither yield ye your members as instruments of unrighteousness unto sin:"

IV. Respond to God

Romans 6:13 "**but yield yourselves unto God,** as those that are alive from the dead, and your members as instruments of righteousness unto God."

I. The Deeds of Self

Romans 7:18 "For I know that **in me** (that is, in my flesh,) **dwelleth no good thing:**"

II. The Desires of Self

Romans 7:18 "for to will is present with me; but how to perform that which is good I find not."

III. The Desperation of Self

Romans 7:19-20 "**For the good that I would I do not: but the evil which I would not, that I do.** [20]Now if I do that I would not, it is no more I that do it, but sin that dwelleth in me."

IV. The Delight through the Spirit

Romans 7:22 "For I delight in the law of God after the inward man: "

I. The Prognosis of Salvation

Romans 8:29 "For whom he did foreknow, he also did predestinate to be conformed to the image of his Son, that he might be the first-born among many brethren."

II. The Purpose of Salvation

Romans 8:29 "For whom he did foreknow, he also did **predestinate to be conformed to the image of his Son,** that he might be the firstborn among many brethren."

III. The Proclamation of Salvation

Romans 8:30 "Moreover **whom he did predestinate, them he also called:** and whom he called, them he also justified: and whom he justified, them he also glorified."

IV. The Purification of Salvation

Romans 8:30 "Moreover whom he did predestinate, them he also called: **and whom he called, them he also justified:** and whom he justified, them he also glorified."

V. The Perfection of Salvation

Romans 8:30 "Moreover whom he did predestinate, them he also called: and whom he called, them he also justified: **and whom he justified, them he also glorified.**"

I. A Burden for Souls

Romans 9:2 "I have great heaviness . . . in my heart."

II. A Brokenness over Souls

Romans 9:2 "I have . . . continual sorrow in my heart."

III. A Bond with Souls

Romans 9:3 "For I could wish that myself were accursed from Christ for my brethren, my kinsmen according to the flesh:"

Souls are perishing. Do you care?

I. The Great Mission - Salvation

Romans 10:1 "my heart's desire and prayer to God for Israel is, that they might be saved."

II. The Great Misconception - Sincerity

Romans 10:2 "they have a zeal of God, but not according to knowledge."

III. The Great Miscalculation - Submission

Roman 10:3 "For **they being ignorant of God's righteousness,** and going about to establish their own righteousness, have not submitted themselves unto the righteousness of God."

IV. The Great Mandate - Surrender

Romans 10:4 "For Christ is the end of the law for righteousness to every one that believeth."

I. The Depth of God's Knowledge

Romans 11:33 "O the depth of the riches both of the wisdom and knowledge of God!"

II. The Diversity of God's Ways

Romans 11:33 "...how unsearchable are his judgments, and his ways past finding out!"

III. The Distinction of God's Competence

Romans 11:34 "For who hath known the mind of the Lord? or who hath been his counsellor"

IV. The Donation of God's Generosity

Romans 11:35 "Or who hath first given to him, and it shall be recompensed unto him again?"

V. The Declaration of God's Supremacy

Romans 11:36 "For of him, and through him, and to him, are all things: to whom be glory for ever. Amen."

I. The Request

Romans 12:1 "I beseech you therefore, brethren, by the mercies of God, that ye **present your bodies...**"

Present - "To stand beside, or to exhibit."

The Levitical priest, when laying a sacrifice on the altar would "present," stand beside, and exhibit that sacrifice before God.

II. The Reason

Romans 12:1 "I beseech you therefore, brethren, **by the mercies of God,** that ye present your bodies..."

Why should we sacrifice our bodies to God? Because of the mercies of God.

III. The Restriction

Romans 12:2 "And **be not conformed to this world...**"

Don't let the world around you squeeze you into its mold.

IV. The Resolution

Romans 12:2 "**but be ye transformed by the renewing of your mind,** that ye may prove what is that good, and acceptable, and perfect, will of God."

You are either being conformed or you are being transformed.

Romans 13:1 "Let every soul be subject unto the higher powers. For there is no power but of God: the powers that be are ordained of God."

I. Who

"Let every soul"

II. What

"be subject"

III. Where

"unto the higher powers"

IV. Why

"For there is no power but of God: the powers that be are ordained of God."

I. The Error of Pre-mature Judgment

Romans 14:10 "But why dost thou judge thy brother? or why dost thou set at nought thy brother?"

II. The Event of Pronounced Judgment

Romans 14:10 "...for we shall all stand before the judgment seat of Christ."

III. The Experience of a Profound Judge

Romans 14:11 "For it is written, As I live, saith the Lord, every knee shall bow to me, and every tongue shall confess to God."

IV. The Explanation before a Perfect Judge

Romans 14:12 "So then every one of us shall give account of himself to God."

V. The Extinguishing of Personal Judgment

Romans 14:13 "Let us not therefore judge one another any more: but judge this rather, that no man put a stumblingblock or an occasion to fall in his brother's way."

I. **The Example of Getting Along**

Romans 5:5 "the God of patience and consolation"

II. **The Energy to Get Along**

Romans 5:5 "grant you to be"

III. **The Exhortation to Get Along**

Romans 5:5 "to be likeminded one toward another according to Christ Jesus:"

IV. **The Essentials of Getting Along**

Romans 5:6 "That ye may with one mind and one mouth glorify God"

Let's determine to be like Christ and strive to dwell together in unity!

I. A Genuine Recommendation

Romans 16:1 "I commend unto you Phebe our sister"

II. A Gracious Recommendation

Romans 16:1 "...which is a servant of the church which is at Cenchrea:"

III. A Generous Recommendation

Romans 16:2 "That ye receive her in the Lord, as becometh saints, and that ye **assist her in whatsoever business she hath need of you:**"

IV. A Grateful Recommendation

Romans 16:2 "...for she hath been a succourer of many, and of myself also."

I. The Unity of Speech

1 Corinthians 1:10 "Now I beseech you, brethren, by the name of our Lord Jesus Christ, **that ye all speak the same thing**"

II. The Uniformity of Sight

1 Corinthians 1:10 "and that there be no divisions among you; but that ye be perfectly **joined together in the same mind and in the same judgment.**"

III. The Ungodliness of Strife

1 Corinthians 1:11 "For it hath been declared unto me of you, my brethren, by them which are of the house of Chloe, **that there are contentions among you.**"

IV. The Unholiness of Sects

1 Corinthians 1:12-13 "[12]Now this I say, that every one of you saith, I am of Paul; and I of Apollos; and I of Cephas; and I of Christ. [13]Is Christ divided? was Paul crucified for you? or were ye baptized in the name of Paul?"

I. Preaching devoid of Showmanship

1 Corinthians 2:1 "And I, brethren, when I came to you, **came not with excellency of speech** or of wisdom, declaring unto you the testimony of God."

II. Preaching that denies Shrewdness

1 Corinthians 2:1 "And I, brethren, when I came to you, came not with excellency of speech **or of wisdom,** declaring unto you the testimony of God."

III. Preaching dependent upon Scripture

1 Corinthians 2:1 "And I, brethren, when I came to you, came not with excellency of speech or of wisdom, **declaring unto you the testimony of God.**"

IV. Preaching that delights in the Savior

1 Corinthians 2:2 "For I determined not to know any thing among you, save Jesus Christ, and him crucified."

I. The Problem - Spiritual Immaturity

1 Corinthians 3:1 "brethren, could not speak unto you as unto spiritual, but as unto carnal, **even as unto babes in Christ.**"

II. The Prognosis - Spiritual Nourishment

1 Corinthians 3:2 "I have fed you with milk, and not with meat: for hitherto ye were not able to bear it, neither yet now are ye able."

III. The Provocations - Envying, Strife, and Divisions

1 Corinthians 3:3 "**For ye are yet carnal:** for whereas there is **among you envying, and strife, and divisions,** are ye not carnal, and walk as men?"

1 Corinthians 4:7 "For who maketh thee to differ from another? and what hast thou that thou didst not receive? now if thou didst receive it, why dost thou glory, as if thou hadst not received it?"

I. Don't Glory in your Positions

"who maketh thee to differ from another"

II. Don't Glory in your Possessions

"and what hast thou that thou didst not receive?"

III. Glory in Your Creator

"For who maketh thee..."

IV. Glory in the Provider

"now if thou didst receive it, why dost thou glory, as if thou hadst not received it?"

I. Public Reproach

1 Corinthians 5:1 "**It is reported commonly that there is fornication among you,** and such fornication as is not so much as named among the Gentiles, that one should have his father's wife."

II. Pompous Revelry

1 Corinthians 5:2 "And **ye are puffed up, and have not rather mourned,** that he that hath done this deed might be taken away from among you."

III. Personal Rebuke

1 Corinthians 5:3 "For I verily, as absent in body, but present in spirit, **have judged already,** as though I were present, concerning him that hath so done this deed,"

IV. Providential Rescue

1 Corinthians 5:5 "**To deliver such an one unto Satan for the destruction of the flesh,** that the spirit may be saved in the day of the Lord Jesus."

V. Pride Reprimanded

1 Corinthians 5:6 "**Your glorying is not good.** Know ye not that a little leaven leaveneth the whole lump?"

1 Corinthians 6:19-20 "What? know ye not that your body is the temple of the Holy Ghost which is in you, which ye have of God, and ye are not your own? [20]For ye are bought with a price: therefore glorify God in your body, and in your spirit, which are God's."

I. The Occupant of the Temple

"know ye not that **your body is the temple of the Holy Ghost** which is in you"

II. The Owner of the Temple

"...which ye have of God, and **ye are not your own**? [20]For ye are bought with a price:"

III. The Occupation of the Temple

"**therefore glorify God in your body,** and in your spirit, which are God's."

1 Corinthians 7:23-24 "[23]Ye are bought with a price; be not ye the servants of men. [24]Brethren, let every man, wherein he is called, therein abide with God."

I. Our Acquisition

"Ye are bought with a price"

II. Our Allegiance

"be not ye the servants of men"

III. Our Association

"Brethren, let every man, wherein he is called, therein abide with God."

1 Corinthians 8:2-3 "[2]And if any man think that he knoweth any thing, he knoweth nothing yet as he ought to know. [3]But if any man love God, the same is known of him."

I. Acknowledgment of our Personal Ignorance

"if any man think that he knoweth any thing, he knoweth nothing yet as he ought to know."

II. Acceptance of a Divine Invitation

"But if any man love God, the same is known of him."

Our worth is not in what we know, but in Who we know!

I. The Run

1 Corinthians 9:24 "Know ye not that they which run in a race run all"

II. The Resolve

1 Corinthians 9:24 So run, that ye may obtain."

III. The Reward

1 Corinthian 9:25 "And every man that striveth for the mastery is temperate in all things. Now they do it to obtain a corruptible crown; **but we an incorruptible.**"

IV. The Response

1 Corinthians 9:26 "**I therefore so run,** not as uncertainly; so fight I, not as one that beateth the air:"

V. The Restraint

1 Corinthians 9:27 "**But I keep under my body, and bring it into subjection:** lest that by any means, when I have preached to others, I myself should be a castaway."

1 Corinthians 10:13 "There hath no temptation taken you but such as is common to man: but God is faithful, who will not suffer you to be tempted above that ye are able; but will with the temptation also make a way to escape, that ye may be able to bear it."

I. The Reality of Temptation

"There hath no temptation taken you but such as is common to man"

II. The Restrictions upon Temptation

"but God is faithful, who will not suffer you to be tempted above that ye are able"

III. The Rescue from Temptation

"but will with the temptation also make a way to escape, that ye may be able to bear it."

I. It's Right to Pursue Godly Men

1 Corinthians 11:1 "Be ye followers of me, even as I also am of Christ."

II. It's Right to Pattern Godly Men

1 Corinthians 11:2 "Now I praise you, brethren, **that ye remember me in all things,** and keep the ordinances, as I delivered them to you."

III. The Right Perspective of Godly Men

1 Corinthians 11:3 "But I would have you know, that **the head of every man is Christ;** and the head of the woman is the man; and the head of Christ is God."

I. The Unity of the Body of Christ

1 Corinthians 12:12 "For as the body is one, and hath many members, **and all the members of that one body, being many, are one body:** so also is Christ."

II. Conformity into the Body of Christ

1 Corinthians 12:13 "**For by one Spirit are we all baptized into one body,** whether we be Jews or Gentiles, whether we be bond or free; and have been all made to drink into one Spirit."

III. The Diversity of the Body of Christ

1 Corinthians 12:14 "For the body is not one member, but many."

IV. The Design of the Body of Christ

1 Corinthians 12:18 "But now hath God set the members every one of them in the body, as it hath pleased him."

I. The Suffering of Love

1 Corinthians 13:4 "Charity suffereth long"

II. The Sincerity of Love

1 Corinthians 13:4 "and is kind; charity envieth not; charity vaunteth not itself, is not puffed up"

III. The Stability of Love

1 Corinthians 13:5 "Doth not behave itself unseemly, seeketh not her own, is not easily provoked, thinketh no evil"

IV. The Sympathy of Love

1 Corinthians 13:6 "Rejoiceth not in iniquity, but rejoiceth in the truth;"

V. The Sacrifice of Love

1 Corinthians 13:7 "Beareth all things, believeth all things, hopeth all things, endureth all things."

I. Her Speech

1 Corinthians 14:34 "Let your women keep silence in the churches: for it is not permitted unto them to speak;"

II. Her Submission

1 Corinthians 14:34 "but they are commanded to be under obedience, as also saith the law."

III. Her Schooling

1 Corinthians 14:35 "And if they will learn any thing, let them ask their husbands at home:"

IV. Her Shame

1 Corinthians 14:35 "for it is a shame for women to speak in the church."

1 Corinthians 15:34 "Awake to righteousness, and sin not; for some have not the knowledge of God: I speak this to your shame."

I. It's Time to Wake Up

"Awake to righteousness"

II. It's Time to Shape Up

"and sin not"

III. It's Time to Pray Up

"for some have not the knowledge of God"

IV. It's Time to Confess Up

"I speak this to your shame."

1 Corinthians 16:13-14 "[13]Watch ye, stand fast in the faith, quit you like men, be strong. [14]Let all your things be done with charity."

I. Be Alert

"Watch ye"

II. Be Assertive

"stand fast in the faith"

III. Be Authoritative

"quit you like men"

IV. Be Aggressive

"be strong"

V. Be Appropriate

"Let all your things be done with charity."

2 Corinthians 1:3-4 "³Blessed be God, even the Father of our Lord Jesus Christ, the Father of mercies, and the God of all comfort; ⁴Who comforteth us in all our tribulation, that we may be able to comfort them which are in any trouble, by the comfort wherewith we ourselves are comforted of God."

I. Praise for the Comforter

"Blessed be God, even the Father of our Lord Jesus Christ, the Father of mercies, and the God of all comfort;"

II. The Period of Comfort

"Who comforteth us in all our tribulation"

III. The Purpose of Comfort

"that we may be able to comfort them which are in any trouble"

IV. The Proceeds of Comfort

"by the comfort wherewith we ourselves are comforted of God."

2 Corinthians 2:10-11 "[10]To whom ye forgive any thing, I forgive also: for if I forgave any thing, to whom I forgave it, for your sakes forgave I it in the person of Christ; [11]Lest Satan should get an advantage of us: for we are not ignorant of his devices."

I. The Message of Forgiveness

"To whom ye forgive any thing, I forgive also:"

II. The Model of Forgiveness

"for if I forgave any thing, to whom I forgave it, for your sakes forgave I it
""

III. The Misfortune of Unforgiveness

"Lest Satan should get an advantage of us: for we are not ignorant of his devices."

2 Corinthians 3:5 "Not that we are sufficient of ourselves to think any thing as of ourselves; but our sufficiency is of God;"

I. Our Inadequacy

"Not that we are sufficient of ourselves"

II. Our Inability

"to think any thing as of ourselves"

III. Our Sufficiency

"but our sufficiency is of God;"

All that I am or ever hope to be, I owe it all to Him!

I. The Priority

2 Corinthians 4:1 "Therefore seeing we have this ministry, as we have received mercy, we faint not;"

II. The Purification

2 Corinthians 4:2 "But have renounced the hidden things of dishonesty, not walking in craftiness, nor handling the word of God deceitfully;"

III. The Preaching

2 Corinthians 4:2 "but by manifestation of the truth commending ourselves to every man's conscience in the sight of God."

IV. The Problem

2 Corinthians 4:3 "But if our gospel be hid, it is hid to them that are lost:"

V. The Provocation

2 Corinthians 4:4 "In whom the god of this world hath blinded the minds of them which believe not, lest the light of the glorious gospel of Christ, who is the image of God, should shine unto them."

I. The Confidence

2 Corinthians 5:6 "Therefore we are always confident, knowing that, whilst we are at home in the body, we are absent from the Lord:"

II. The Commitment

2 Corinthians 5:7 "(For we walk by faith, not by sight:)"

III. The Certainty

2 Corinthians 5:8 "We are confident, I say, and willing rather to be absent from the body, and to be present with the Lord."

IV. The Commendation

2 Corinthians 5:9 "Wherefore we labour, that, whether present or absent, we may be accepted of him."

V. The Checkup

2 Corinthians 5:10 "For we must all appear before the judgment seat of Christ; that every one may receive the things done in his body, according to that he hath done, whether it be good or bad."

2 Corinthians 6:1 "We then, as workers together with him, beseech you also that ye receive not the grace of God in vain."

I. Our Privilege

"We then, as workers together with him"

II. Our Passion

"beseech you also"

III. Our Passivity

"that ye receive not the grace of God in vain."

2 Corinthians 7:1 "Having therefore these promises, dearly beloved, let us cleanse ourselves from all filthiness of the flesh and spirit, perfecting holiness in the fear of God."

I. Acceptance of God's Word

"Having therefore these promises"

II. Appreciation of God's Word

"let us cleanse ourselves from all filthiness of the flesh and spirit"

III. Application of God's Word

"perfecting holiness in the fear of God"

I. The Secret of this Church

2 Corinthians 8:1 "...we do you to wit of **the grace of God** bestowed on the churches of Macedonia;"

II. The Suffering of this Church

2 Corinthians 8:2 "How that in a **great trial of affliction** the abundance of their joy and their deep poverty abounded unto the riches of their liberality."

III. The Sacrifice of this Church

2 Corinthians 8:3 "For **to their power,** I bear record, yea, **and beyond their power** they were willing of themselves;"

IV. The Steadfastness of this Church

2 Corinthians 8:4 "Praying us **with much entreaty** that we would receive the gift, and take upon us the fellowship of the ministering to the saints."

V. The Surrender of this Church

2 Corinthians 8:5"And this they did, not as we hoped, **but first gave their own selves to the Lord,** and unto us by the will of God."

I. A Principle that Excites

2 Corinthians 9:6 "He which soweth sparingly shall reap also sparingly; and he which soweth bountifully shall reap also bountifully."

II. A Purpose to Embrace

2 Corinthians 9:7 "Every man according as he purposeth in his heart"

III. A Passion to Enjoy

2 Corinthians 9:7 "so let him give; not grudgingly, or of necessity: for God loveth a cheerful giver."

IV. A Promise to Expect

2 Corinthians 9:8 "And God is able to make all grace abound toward you; that ye, always having all sufficiency in all things, may abound to every good work:"

2 Corinthians 10:12-13 "¹²For we dare not make ourselves of the number, or compare ourselves with some that commend themselves: but they measuring themselves by themselves, and comparing themselves among themselves, are not wise. ¹³But we will not boast of things without our measure, but according to the measure of the rule which God hath distributed to us, a measure to reach even unto you."

I. A Faulty Comparison

"compare ourselves with some that commend themselves:"

II. A Foolish Comparison

"but they measuring themselves by themselves, and comparing themselves among themselves, are not wise."

III. A Faithful Comparison

"but according to the measure of the rule which God hath distributed to us, a measure to reach even unto you."

2 Corinthians 11:3 "But I fear, lest by any means, as the serpent beguiled Eve through his subtilty, so your minds should be corrupted from the simplicity that is in Christ."

I. A Concern

"But I fear"

II. A Casualty

"lest by any means, as the serpent beguiled Eve through his subtilty"

III. A Corruption

"so your minds should be corrupted"

IV. A Cause

"from the simplicity that is in Christ."

I. The Benefit of Burdens

2 Corinthians 12:7 "And **lest I should be exalted above measure** through the abundance of the revelations, there was given to me a thorn in the flesh, the messenger of Satan to buffet me, lest I should be exalted above measure."

II. The Bestowment of Burdens

2 Corinthians 12:7 "And lest I should be exalted above measure through the abundance of the revelations, **there was given to me** a thorn in the flesh, the messenger of Satan to buffet me, lest I should be exalted above measure."

III. The Bearer of Burdens

2 Corinthians 12:7 "And lest I should be exalted above measure through the abundance of the revelations, **there was given to me a thorn in the flesh, the messenger of Satan to buffet me,** lest I should be exalted above measure."

IV. The Blessing of Burdens

2 Corinthians 12:9 "And he said unto me, **My grace is sufficient for thee: for my strength is made perfect in weakness.** Most gladly therefore will I rather glory in my infirmities, that the power of Christ may rest upon me.

2 Corinthians 13:11 "Finally, brethren, farewell. Be perfect, be of good comfort, be of one mind, live in peace; and the God of love and peace shall be with you."

I. Be Grounded

"Be perfect"

II. Be Gracious

"be of good comfort"

III. Be Governed

"be of one mind"

IV. Be Gentle

"live in peace"

V. Be Godly

"and the God of love and peace shall be with you"

Galatians 1:10 "For do I now persuade men, or God? or do I seek to please men? for if I yet pleased men, I should not be the servant of Christ."

I. What are You Living For?

"do I now persuade men, or God?"

II. What are you Longing For?

"do I seek to please men?"

III. What are you Loving Most?

"for if I yet pleased men, I should not be the servant of Christ."

Galatians 2:21 "I do not frustrate the grace of God: for if righteousness come by the law, then Christ is dead in vain."

I. Rules don't Establish a Relationship

"I do not frustrate the grace of God:"

II. Rules don't Equal Righteousness

"for if righteousness come by the law"

III. Rules don't Equate Redemption

"then Christ is dead in vain."

Galatians 3:1 "O foolish Galatians, who hath bewitched you, that ye should not obey the truth, before whose eyes Jesus Christ hath been evidently set forth, crucified among you?"

I. **Bewitched by Deception**

"**O foolish Galatians,**"

II. **Bewitched by Disobedience**

"who hath bewitched you, **that ye should not obey the truth**"

III. **Bewitched by Denial**

"before whose eyes Jesus Christ hath been **evidently set forth**"

Galatians 4:19 "My little children, of whom I travail in birth again until Christ be formed in you,"

I. **Serious about Your Soul**

"My little children"

II. **Serious about Your Spiritual Success**

"of whom I travail in birth again"

III. **Serious about Your Sanctification**

"until Christ be formed in you,"

Galatians 5:1 "Stand fast therefore in the liberty wherewith Christ hath made us free, and be not entangled again with the yoke of bondage."

I. The Privilege of Freedom

"Stand fast therefore in the liberty"

II. The Pathway to Freedom

"wherewith Christ hath made us free,"

III. The Prevention of Freedom

"and be not entangled again with the yoke of bondage."

There is freedom from every sin through Jesus Christ!

I. Don't give in to Sin

Galatians 6:7 "Be not deceived; God is not mocked: for whatsoever a man soweth, that shall he also reap."

II. Don't Give Up in Service

Galatians 6: 9 "And let us not be weary in well doing: for in due season we shall reap, if we faint not."

III. Don't Give Out in Sharing

Galatians 6:10 "As we have therefore opportunity, let us do good unto all men, especially unto them who are of the household of faith."

I. **I Praise the Lord for Your Faith**

Ephesians 1:15 "Wherefore I also, after **I heard of your faith in the Lord Jesus,** and love unto all the saints,"

II. **I Praise the Lord for Your Fellowship**

Ephesians 1:15 "Wherefore I also, after I heard of your faith in the Lord Jesus, **and love unto all the saints,**"

III. **I Pray to the Lord for You Faithfully**

Ephesians 1:16 "Cease not to give thanks for you, making mention of you in my prayers"

IV. **I Pray to the Lord for Your Future**

Ephesians 1:17 "That the God of our Lord Jesus Christ, the Father of glory, may give unto you the spirit of wisdom and revelation in the knowledge of him:"

Friends pray for their friends. Who have you prayed for today?

I. Our Past

Ephesians 2:5 "Even **when we were dead in sins,** hath quickened us together with Christ, (by grace ye are saved;)"

II. Our Present

Ephesians 2:6 "And hath raised us up together, and **made us sit together in heavenly places in Christ Jesus:**"

III. Our Future

Ephesians 2:7 "That in the ages to come he might shew the exceeding riches of his grace in his kindness toward us through Christ Jesus."

Ephesians 3:16 "That he would grant you, according to the riches of his glory, to be strengthened with might by his Spirit in the inner man;"

I. The Supply of Our God

"according to the riches of his glory"

II. The Strength of Our God

"to be strengthened with might"

III. The Spirit of Our God

"by his Spirit"

IV. The Sufficiency of Our God

"in the inner man"

I. Our Association

Ephesians 4:1 "I therefore, **the prisoner of the Lord,** beseech you that ye walk worthy of the vocation wherewith ye are called,"

II. Our Vocation

Ephesians 4:1 "I therefore, the prisoner of the Lord, beseech you that ye **walk worthy of the vocation wherewith ye are called,**"

III. Our Consecration

Ephesians 4:2 "With all lowliness and meekness, with longsuffering, forbearing one another in love;"

IV. Our Unification

"Endeavouring to keep the unity of the Spirit in the bond of peace."

I. A Word about Commitment

Ephesians 5:1 "Be ye therefore followers of God, as dear children;"

II. A Word about Compassion

Ephesians 5:2 "And **walk in love, as Christ also hath loved us,** and hath given himself for us an offering and a sacrifice to God for a sweetsmelling savour."

III. A Word about Cleanliness

Ephesians 5:3 "But fornication, and all uncleanness, or covetousness, let it not be once named among you, as becometh saints;"

IV. A Word about Communication

Ephesians 5:4 "Neither filthiness, nor foolish talking, nor jesting, which are not convenient: but rather giving of thanks."

I. **What Parents should Require of their Children**

   A. Obedience

   Ephesians 6:1 "Children, **obey your parents in the Lord:** for this is right."

   B. Respect

   Ephesians 6:2 "**Honour they father and mother;** which is the first commandment of promise;"

II. **How Parents should Respond to their Children**

   Ephesians 6:4 "And, ye fathers, **provoke not your children to wrath...**"

III. **What Parents should Reflect Before their Children**

   Ephesians 6:4 "And, ye fathers, provoke not your children to wrath: but **bring them up in the nurture and admonition of the Lord.**"

Philippians 1:1 "Paul and Timotheus, the servants of Jesus Christ, to all the saints in Christ Jesus which are at Philippi, with the bishops and deacons:"

I. The Ministers

"Paul and Timotheus"

II. The Mission

"servants"

III. The Master

"Jesus Christ"

IV. The Ministry

"all the saints in Christ Jesus which are at Philippi,"

I. **The Admonition to Reject Selfishness**

Philippians 2:3 "**Let nothing be done through strife or vainglory;** but in lowliness of mind let each esteem other better than themselves."

II. **The Advice to Relish Service**

Philippians 2:3 "Let nothing be done through strife or vainglory; but **in lowliness of mind let each esteem other better than themselves.**"

III. **The Attribute that Reflects the Savior**

Philippians 2:4 "Look not every man on his own things, but every man also on the things of others."

Philippians 3:9 "And be found in him, not having mine own righteousness, which is of the law, but that which is through the faith of Christ, the righteousness which is of God by faith:"

I. The Find

"And be found in him"

II. The Failure

"not having mine own righteousness, which is of the law"

III. The Faith

"but that which is through the faith of Christ"

IV. The Father

"the righteousness which is of God by faith:"

Philippians 4:4 "Rejoice in the Lord alway: and again I say, Rejoice."

I. The Command of Rejoicing

"Rejoice"

II. The Cause for Rejoicing

"in the Lord"

III. The Consistency of Rejoicing

"alway"

IV. The Commitment to Rejoicing

"and again I say, Rejoice"

I. He is the First

Colossians 1:17 "**And he is before all things,** and by him all things consist."

II. He is the Founder

Colossians 1:17 "And he is before all things, and **by him all things consist.**"

III. He is the Foreman

Colossians 1:18 "And **he is the head of the body,** the church: who is the beginning, the firstborn from the dead; that in all things he might have the preeminence."

IV. He is the Firstborn

Colossians 1:18 "And he is the head of the body, the church: who is the beginning, **the firstborn from the dead;** that in all things he might have the preeminence."

V. He is the Foremost

Colossians 1:18 "And he is the head of the body, the church: who is the beginning, the firstborn from the dead; that **in all things he might have the preeminence.**"

I. **Salvation**

Colossians 2:6 "As ye have therefore received Christ Jesus the Lord, so walk ye in him:"

II. **Surrender**

Colossians 2:6 "As ye have therefore received Christ Jesus the Lord, **so walk ye in him:**"

III. **Secure**

Colossians 2:7 "**Rooted and built up in him, and stablished in the faith,** as ye have been taught, abounding therein with thanksgiving."

IV. **Satisfied**

Colossians 2:7 "Rooted and built up in him, and stablished in the faith, as ye have been taught, **abounding therein with thanksgiving.**"

Colossians 3:4 "When Christ, who is our life, shall appear, then shall ye also appear with him in glory."

I. Our Savior

"Christ"

II. Our Sustainer

"who is our life"

III. Our Surety

"shall appear"

IV. Our Sufficiency

"then shall ye also appear with him in glory."

I. **Pray for the Witness of Your Pastor**

Colossians 4:3 " Withal praying also for us, **that God would open unto us a door of utterance, to speak the mystery of Christ,** for which I am also in bonds:"

II. **Pray for the Welfare of Your Pastor**

Colossians 4:3 "Withal praying also for us, that God would open unto us a door of utterance, to speak the mystery of Christ, **for which I am also in bonds:**"

III. **Pray for Wisdom for Your Pastor**

Colossians 4:4 "**That I may make it manifest,** as I ought to speak."

I. This was a Working Church

I Thessalonians 1:3 "Remembering without ceasing **your work of faith, and labour of love,** and patience of hope in our Lord Jesus Christ . . . "

II. This was a Worshiping Church

I Thessalonians 1:5 "For our gospel came not unto you in word only, but also in power, and in the Holy Ghost, and in much assurance..."

III. This was a Witnessing Church

I Thessalonians 1:8 "For **from you sounded out the word of the Lord** not only in Macedonia and Achaia, but also in every place your faith to god-ward is spread abroad; so that we need not to speak any thing."

IV. This was a Watching Church

I Thessalonians 1:10 "And **to wait for his Son from heaven,** whom he raised from the dead, even Jesus, which delivered us from the wrath to come."

1 Thessalonians 2:13 "For this cause also thank we God without ceasing, because, when ye received the word of God which ye heard of us, ye received it not as the word of men, but as it is in truth, the word of God, which effectually worketh also in you that believe."

I. The Reception of the Word

"ye received the word of God...ye received it"

II. The Reverance of the Word

"not as the word of men,"

III. The Reformation by the Word

"which effectually worketh also in you"

IV. The Responsibility to the Word

"that believe."

I. A Model Pastor is Persistent

"Night and day"

II. A Model Pastor is Prayerful

"praying exceedingly "

III. A Model Pastor is Personable

"that we might see your face"

IV. A Model Pastor is Purposeful

"and might perfect that which is lacking in your faith?"

I. **Listen with Constraint**

1 Thessalonians 4:11 "And that ye **study to be quiet,** and to do your own business, and to work with your own hands, as we commanded you;"

II. **Labor with Confidence**

1 Thessalonians 4:11 "And that ye study to be quiet, and to do your own business, and to **work with your own hands,** as we commanded you;"

III. **Live with Conscience**

1 Thessalonians 4:12 "That ye may **walk honestly toward them that are without,** and that ye may have lack of nothing."

I. Be Joyful

1 Thessalonians 5:16 "Rejoice evermore."

II. Be Prayerful

1 Thessalonians 5:17 "Pray without ceasing."

III. Be Thankful

1 Thessalonians 5:18 "In every thing give thanks: for this is the will of God in Christ Jesus concerning you."

I. I'm Proud of Your Spiritual Progress

2 Thessalonians 1:3 "We are bound to thank God always for you, brethren, as it is meet, because that **your faith groweth exceedingly,** and the charity of every one of you all toward each other aboundeth;"

II. I'm Proud of Your Sacrificial Passion

2 Thessalonians 1:3 "We are bound to thank God always for you, brethren, as it is meet, because that your faith groweth exceedingly, and **the charity of every one of you all toward each other aboundeth;**"

III. I'm Proud of Your Steadfast Persistence

2 Thessalonians 1:4 "So that we ourselves glory in you in the churches of God for your patience and faith in all your persecutions and tribulations that ye endure:"

2 Thessalonians 2:14 "Whereunto he called you by our gospel, to the obtaining of the glory of our Lord Jesus Christ."

I. The Sovereignty of God

"Whereunto he called you"

II. The Responsibility of Man

"by our gospel"

III. The Glory of God

"to the obtaining of the glory of our Lord Jesus Christ."

2 Thessalonians 3:3 "But the Lord is faithful, who shall stablish you, and keep you from evil."

I. Our God is Dependable

"the Lord is faithful"

II. Our God is a Developer

"who shall stablish you"

III. Our God is a Defender

"and keep you from evil."

1 Timothy 1:5 "Now the end of the commandment is charity out of a pure heart, and of a good conscience, and of faith unfeigned:"

I. Charity to All

"the end of the commandment is charity"

II. Purity to God

"of a pure heart"

III. Integrity to Man

"and of a good conscience"

IV. Spirituality to Christ

"and of faith unfeigned"

I. The Pattern of Prayer

1 Timothy 2:1 "I exhort therefore, that, first of all, **supplications, prayers, intercessions, and giving of thanks,** be made for all men;"

II. The People of Prayer

1 Timothy 2:1-2 "be made **for all men**; ²**For kings, and for all that are in authority**; that we may lead a quiet and peaceable life in all godliness and honesty."

III. The Peace of Prayer

1 Timothy 2:2b "**that we may lead a quiet and peaceable life in all godliness and honesty.**"

IV. The Plan of Prayer

1 Timothy 2:3-4 "For this is good and acceptable in the sight of God our Saviour; ⁴ Who will have all men to be saved, and to come unto the knowledge of the truth."

V. The Priority of Prayer

1 Timothy 2:8 "I will therefore that men pray every where, lifting up holy hands, without wrath and doubting."

1 Timothy 3:13 "For they that have used the office of a deacon well purchase to themselves a good degree, and great boldness in the faith which is in Christ Jesus."

I. A Deacon's Commitment

"they that have used the office of a deacon well"

II. A Deacon's Consecration

"purchase to themselves a good degree"

III. A Deacon's Confidence

and great boldness in the faith"

1 Timothy 4:16 "Take heed unto thyself, and unto the doctrine; continue in them: for in doing this thou shalt both save thyself, and them that hear thee."

I. Make Your Spirituality a Priority

"Take heed unto thyself"

II. Make the Scriptures a Priority

"and unto the doctrine"

III. Make Steadfastness a Priority

"continue in them:"

IV. Make Shepherding a Priority

"for in doing this thou shalt both save thyself, and them that hear thee."

1 Timothy 5:22 "Lay hands suddenly on no man, neither be partaker of other men's sins: keep thyself pure."

I. Be Patient with People

"Lay hands suddenly on no man"

II. Be Prudent with People

"neither be partaker of other men's sins"

III. Be Pure with People

"keep thyself pure."

1 Timothy 6:1 "Let as many servants as are under the yoke count their own masters worthy of all honour, that the name of God and his doctrine be not blasphemed."

I. The Turmoil

"many servants as are under the yoke"

II. The Task

"count their own masters worthy of all honour"

III. The Theology

"that the name of God and his doctrine be not blasphemed."

2 Timothy 1:7 "For God hath not given us the spirit of fear; but of power, and of love, and of a sound mind."

I. **No Fear - because You have God's Power that Protects You**

   "but of power,"

II. **No Fear - because You have God's Love that Accepts You**

   "and of love,"

III. **No Fear - because You have God's Wisdom that Directs You**

   "and of a sound mind."

2 Timothy 2:2 "And the things that thou hast heard of me among many witnesses, the same commit thou to faithful men, who shall be able to teach others also."

I. The Things You've Been Given You Need to Get

"things that thou hast heard of me among many witnesses"

II. The Things You Get, You Need to Give

"the same commit thou to faithful men"

III. The People to Whom You Give Need to Get Giving

"who shall be able to teach others also."

2 Timothy 3:8 "Now as Jannes and Jambres withstood Moses, so do these also resist the truth: men of corrupt minds, reprobate concerning the faith."

I. Trouble Makers in the Church Persecute Preaching

"resist the truth"

II. Trouble Makers in the Church Promote Pollution

"men of corrupt minds"

III. Trouble Makers in the Church Publicize Perversion

"reprobate concerning the faith"

2 Timothy 3:16-17 "All scripture is given by inspiration of God, and is profitable for doctrine, for reproof, for correction, for instruction in righteousness: [17] That the man of God may be perfect, thoroughly furnished unto all good works."

I. The Author of the Bible

"All scripture is given by inspiration of God"

II. The Authority of the Bible

"and is profitable"

III. The Alteration by the Bible

"may be perfect, thoroughly furnished unto all good works."

I. Demas a Testimony of Failure

2 Timonty 4:10 "For Demas hath forsaken me, having loved this present world, and is departed unto Thessalonica; Crescens to Galatia, Titus unto Dalmatia."

II. Luke a Testimony of Faithfulness

2 Timothy 4:11 "**Only Luke is with me.** Take Mark, and bring him with thee: for he is profitable to me for the ministry. "

III. Mark a Testimony of Forgiveness

2 Timothy 4:11 "Only Luke is with me. Take Mark, and bring him with thee: for **he is profitable to me for the ministry. "**

IV. Paul a Testimony of Frailty

2 Timothy 4:13-14 "The cloke that I left at Troas with Carpus, when thou comest, bring with thee, and the books, but especially the parchments. [14] Alexander the coppersmith did me much evil: the Lord reward him according to his works:"

I. Religious Sinners have a Defiled Will

Titus 1:15 "Unto the pure all things are pure: but unto them that are defiled and unbelieving is nothing pure; but even their mind and conscience is defiled."

II. Religious Sinners have a Defective Walk

Titus 1:16 " They profess that they know God; but **in works they deny him,** being abominable, and disobedient, and unto every good work reprobate."

III. Religious Sinners have a Damaged Witness

Titus 1:16 "They profess that they know God; but in works they deny him, **being abominable, and disobedient, and unto every good work reprobate."**

Titus 2:14 "Who gave himself for us, that he might redeem us from all iniquity, and purify unto himself a peculiar people, zealous of good works."

I. The Message of Substitution

"Who gave himself for us"

II. The Message of Sacrifice

"he might redeem us from all iniquity"

III. The Message of Sanctification

"and purify unto himself a peculiar people, zealous of good works."

Titus 3:5 "Not by works of righteousness which we have done, but according to his mercy he saved us, by the washing of regeneration, and renewing of the Holy Ghost;"

I. The Mistake of Salvation

"Not by works of righteousness which we have done"

II. The Message of Salvation

"according to his mercy he saved us"

III. The Method of Salvation

"by the washing of regeneration, and renewing of the Holy Ghost;"

Philemon 1:3 "Grace to you, and peace, from God our Father and the Lord Jesus Christ."

I. I'm Thankful for God's Favor

"Grace to you"

II. I'm Thankful for God's Friendship

"and peace"

III. I'm Thankful for God's Family

"from God our Father and the Lord Jesus Christ."

Hebrews 1:3 "Who being the brightness of his glory, and the express image of his person, and upholding all things by the word of his power, when he had by himself purged our sins, sat down on the right hand of the Majesty on high;"

I. Jesus Deity is seen in his Person

"Who being the brightness of his glory, and the express image of his person"

II. Jesus Deity is seen in his Power

"and upholding all things by the word of his power"

III. Jesus Deity is seen in his Propitiation

"when he had by himself purged our sins"

IV. Jesus Deity is seen in his Position

"sat down on the right hand of the Majesty on high"

Hebrews 2:1 "Therefore we ought to give the more earnest heed to the things which we have heard, lest at any time we should let them slip."

I. Remember the Truths of Scripture

"we ought to give the more earnest heed to the things which we have heard"

II. Revere the Truths of Scripture

"more earnest heed"

III. Represent the Truths of Scripture

"lest at any time we should let them slip."

I. The Responsibility of Every Believer

Hebrews 2:1 "Therefore we ought to give the more earnest heed to the things which we have heard, lest at any time we should let them slip."

II. The Risk of Every Believer

Hebrews 2:1 "Therefore we ought to give the more earnest heed to the things which we have heard, lest at any time we should let them slip."

III. The Reckoning of Every Believer

Hebrews 2:2-3 "For if the word spoken by angels was stedfast, and every transgression and disobedience received a just recompence of reward; 3 How shall we escape, if we neglect so great salvation; which at the first began to be spoken by the Lord, and was confirmed unto us by them that heard him;

Hebrews 3:10 "Wherefore I was grieved with that generation, and said, They do alway err in their heart; and they have not known my ways."

I. There is a Problem with their Habits

"do alway err"

II. There is a Problem in their Heart

"in their heart"

III. There is a Problem in their Head

"and they have not known my ways"

Hebrews 4:9 "There remaineth therefore a rest to the people of God."

I. It is a Constant Peace

"There remaineth"

II. It is a Comfortable Peace

"a rest"

III. It is a Conditional Peace

"to the people of God."

I. **What You are Missing**

Hebrews 5:11 "Of whom we have many things to say, and hard to be uttered, **seeing ye are dull of hearing.**"

II. **Where you Should be**

Hebrews 5:12 "For when **for the time ye ought to be teachers,** ye have need that one teach you again which be the first principles of the oracles of God; and are become such as have need of milk, and not of strong meat."

III. **What you Need**

Hebrews 5:12 "For when for the time ye ought to be teachers, **ye have need that one teach you again which be the first principles of the oracles of God;** and are become such as have need of milk, and not of strong meat."

IV. **Where you Are**

Hebrews 5:12-13 "[12]For when for the time ye ought to be teachers, ye have need that one teach you again which be the first principles of the oracles of God; **and are become such as have need of milk, and not of strong meat.** [13]**For every one that useth milk is unskilful in the word of righteousness:** for he is a babe."

Hebrews 6:10 "For God is not unrighteous to forget your work and labour of love, which ye have shewed toward his name, in that ye have ministered to the saints, and do minister."

I. God Remembers Your Work

"God is not unrighteous to forget your work and labour of love"

II. God Remembers Your Witnessing

"which ye have shewed toward his name"

III. God Remembers Your Welfare

"in that ye have ministered to the saints, and do minister."

Hebrews 7:19 "For the law made nothing perfect, but the bringing in of a better hope did; by the which we draw nigh unto God."

I. The Law that Condemns

"For the law made nothing perfect"

II. The Hope that Cures

"the bringing in of a better hope did"

III. The Gospel that Connects

"by the which we draw nigh unto God."

Hebrews 8:8 "Now of the things which we have spoken this is the sum: We have such an high priest, who is set on the right hand of the throne of the Majesty in the heavens."

I. The Conclusion of the Matter

"this is the sum:"

II. The Conqueror in the Matter

"We have such an high priest,"

Hebrews 8:12 "For I will be merciful to their unrighteousness, and their sins and their iniquities will I remember no more."

I. I am BLESSED by the Mercy of God

"I will be merciful to their unrighteousness"

II. I am BLESSED by the Memory of God

"their sins and their iniquities will I remember no more."

Hebrews 9:28 "So Christ was once offered to bear the sins of many; and unto them that look for him shall he appear the second time without sin unto salvation."

I. A Stipulation for Sinners

Hebrews 9:27 "**And as it is appointed unto men once to die, but after this the judgment:**"

II. A Substitute for our Sin

Hebrews 9:28 "So Christ was once offered to bear the sins of many; and unto them that look for him shall he appear the second time without sin unto salvation. **Christ was once offered to bear the sins of many**"

III. A Savior for our Salvation

Hebrews 9:28 "So Christ was once offered to bear the sins of many; **and unto them that look for him shall he appear the second time without sin unto salvation.**"

Hebrews 10:14 "For by one offering he hath perfected for ever them that are sanctified."

I. The Perfection of Christ's Gift

"For by one offering he hath perfected"

II. The Permanence of Christ's Gift

"for ever"

III. The People of Christ's Gift

"them that are sanctified."

I. The Response of Faith

Hebrews 11:5 "**By faith Enoch** was translated that he should not see death; and was not found, because God had translated him: for before his translation he had this testimony, that he pleased God."

II. The Recognition of Faith

Hebrews 11:5 "By faith Enoch **was translated that he should not see death;** and was not found, because God had translated him: for before his translation he had this testimony, that he pleased God."

III. The Requirement of Faith

Hebrews 11:6 "But **without faith it is impossible to please him:** for he that cometh to God must believe that he is, and that he is a rewarder of them that diligently seek him."

IV. The Reward of Faith

Hebrews 11:6 "But without faith it is impossible to please him: for he that cometh to God must believe that he is, and that **he is a rewarder of them that diligently seek him.**"

Hebrews 12:1 "Wherefore seeing we also are compassed about with so great a cloud of witnesses, let us lay aside every weight, and the sin which doth so easily beset us, and let us run with patience the race that is set before us,"

I. The Runner's Support

"Wherefore seeing we also are compassed about with so great a cloud of witnesses"

II. The Runner's Strategy

"let us lay aside every weight"

III. The Runner's Seduction

"the sin which doth so easily beset us"

IV. The Runner's Stamina

"let us run with patience the race that is set before us,"

Hebrews 13:5 "Let your conversation be without covetousness; and be content with such things as ye have: for he hath said, I will never leave thee, nor forsake thee."

I. A Concern about Covetousness

"Let your conversation be without covetousness"

II. A Command about Contentment

"and be content with such things as ye have:"

III. A Confidence about Christ

"for he hath said, I will never leave thee, nor forsake thee."

I. Real Religion is Seen in Your Conversation

James 1:26 "If any man among you seem to be religious, **and bridleth not his tongue,** but deceiveth his own heart, this man's religion is vain."

II. Real Religion is Seen in your Compassion

James 1:27 "Pure religion and undefiled before God and the Father is this, **To visit the fatherless and widows in their affliction,** and to keep himself unspotted from the world."

III. Real Religion is Seen in your Conduct

James 1:27 "Pure religion and undefiled before God and the Father is this, To visit the fatherless and widows in their affliction, and **to keep himself unspotted from the world.**"

I. The Demand of Righteousness

James 2:10 "For **whosoever shall keep the whole law,** and yet offend in one point, he is guilty of all."

II. The Downfall of Rebellion

James 2:10 "For whosoever shall keep the whole law, and **yet offend in one point,** he is guilty of all."

III. The Destruction of the Rebellious

James 2:10-11 "[10]For whosoever shall keep the whole law, and yet offend in one point, he is guilty of all. [11]For he that said, Do not commit adultery, said also, Do not kill. **Now if thou commit no adultery, yet if thou kill, thou art become a transgressor of the law.**"

James 3:13 "Who is a wise man and endued with knowledge among you? let him shew out of a good conversation his works with meekness of wisdom."

I. A Wise Man is Seen in his Conversation

"let him shew out of a good conversation"

II. A Wise Man is Seen in his Conduct

"his works"

III. A Wise Man is Seen in his Control

"with meekness of wisdom"

James 4:4 "Ye adulterers and adulteresses, know ye not that the friend-ship of the world is enmity with God? whosoever therefore will be a friend of the world is the enemy of God."

I. The Charge

"Ye adulterers and adulteresses"

II. The Complaint

"know ye not that the friendship of the world is enmity with God?"

III. The Correction

"whosoever therefore will be a friend of the world is the enemy of God."

James 5:8 "Be ye also patient; stablish your hearts: for the coming of the Lord draweth nigh."

I. Be Patient

"Be ye also patient"

II. Be Pure

"stablish your hearts"

III. Be Prepared

"for the coming of the Lord draweth nigh."

1 Peter 1:7 "That the trial of your faith, being much more precious than of gold that perisheth, though it be tried with fire, might be found unto praise and honour and glory at the appearing of Jesus Christ:"

I. The Trouble with Your Trial

"the trial of your faith"

II. The Treasure of Your Trial

"being much more precious than of gold that perisheth"

III. The Testimony of Your Trial

"might be found unto praise and honour and glory at the appearing of Jesus Christ:"

1 Peter 2:9 "But ye are a chosen generation, a royal priesthood, an holy nation, a peculiar people; that ye should shew forth the praises of him who hath called you out of darkness into his marvellous light:"

I. You're Selected

"ye are a chosen generation"

II. You're Special

"a royal priesthood"

III. You're Set Apart

"an holy nation, a peculiar people;"

IV. You're Shining

"that ye should shew forth the praises of him who hath called you out of darkness into his marvellous light:"

1 Peter 3:8 "Finally, be ye all of one mind, having compassion one of another, love as brethren, be pitiful, be courteous:"

I. Christ-Like Concern

"be ye all of one mind"

II. Christ-Like Compassion

"having compassion one of another,"

III. Christ-Like Connections

"be pitiful,"

II. Christ-Like Courtesy

"be courteous,"

1 Peter 4:7 "But the end of all things is at hand: be ye therefore sober, and watch unto prayer."

I. Time is Short

"the end of all things is at hand"

II. Time to get Serious

"be ye therefore sober"

III. Time to Seek God

"and watch unto prayer."

The Blessing of Suffering

I. Suffering Brings Purity

1 Peter 4:12 "Beloved, think it not strange concerning the fiery trial which is to try you, as though some **strange thing happened unto you:**"

II. Suffering Brings Partnership

1 Peter 4:13 "But rejoice, inasmuch as **ye are partakers of Christ's sufferings;** that, when his glory shall be revealed, ye may be glad also with exceeding joy."

III. Suffering Brings Promotion

1 Peter 4:13 "But rejoice, inasmuch as ye are partakers of Christ's sufferings; that, **when his glory shall be revealed, ye may be glad** also with exceeding joy.

III. Suffering Brings Power

1 Peter 4:14 "If ye be reproached for the name of Christ, happy are ye; for the spirit of glory and of God resteth upon you: on their part he is evil spoken of, but on your part he is glorified."

1 Peter 5:5 "Likewise, ye younger, submit yourselves unto the elder. Yea, all of you be subject one to another, and be clothed with humility: for God resisteth the proud, and giveth grace to the humble."

I. Be Submissive

"ye younger, submit yourselves unto the elder"

II. Be Subservient

"Yea, all of you be subject one to another"

III. Be Sincere

"be clothed with humility"

IV. Be Spiritual

"God resisteth the proud, and giveth grace to the humble."

2 Peter 1:4 "Whereby are given unto us exceeding great and precious promises: that by these ye might be partakers of the divine nature, having escaped the corruption that is in the world through lust."

I. The Size of the Gift

"Whereby are given unto us exceeding great and precious promises:"

II. The Superiority of the Gift

"that by these ye might be partakers of the divine nature"

III. The Seriousness of the Gift

"having escaped the corruption that is in the world through lust."

2 Peter 2:10 "But chiefly them that walk after the flesh in the lust of uncleanness, and despise government. Presumptuous are they, selfwilled, they are not afraid to speak evil of dignities."

I. **Worldliness is seen in your Walk**

"them that walk after the flesh in the lust of uncleanness"

II. **Worldliness is seen in your Ways**

"and despise government"

III. **Worldliness is seen in your Work**

"Presumptuous are they"

IV. **Worldliness is seen in your Will**

"selfwilled"

V. **Worldliness is seen in your Words**

"they are not afraid to speak evil of dignities."

2 Peter 3:9 "The Lord is not slack concerning his promise, as some men count slackness; but is longsuffering to us-ward, not willing that any should perish, but that all should come to repentance."

I. The Promises of God

"The Lord is not slack concerning his promise"

II. The Patience of God

"but is longsuffering to us-ward"

III. The Preference of God

"not willing that any should perish, but that all should come to repentance."

1 John 1:9 "If we confess our sins, he is faithful and just to forgive us our sins, and to cleanse us from all unrighteousness."

I. The Realization of Sin

"our sins"

II. The Remedy for Sin

"confess"

III. The Release from Sin

"he is faithful and just to forgive us our sins"

IV. The Removal of Sin

"and to cleanse us from all unrighteousness."

1 John 2:9 "He that saith he is in the light, and hateth his brother, is in darkness even until now."

I. A Proclamation

"He that saith he is in the light"

II. A Problem

"and hateth his brother"

III. A Pronouncement

"is in darkness even until now."

1 John 3:1 "Behold, what manner of love the Father hath bestowed upon us, that we should be called the sons of God: therefore the world knoweth us not, because it knew him not."

I. Realize God's Resolve for You

"Behold, what manner of love the Father hath bestowed upon us"

II. Remember God's Relationship with You

"that we should be called the sons of God"

III. Recognize the Worlds Rejection of You

"therefore the world knoweth us not, because it knew him not."

1 John 4:1 "Beloved, believe not every spirit, but try the spirits whether they are of God: because many false prophets are gone out into the world."

I. Be Cautious

"Beloved, believe not every spirit"

II. Be Careful

"but try the spirits whether they are of God:"

III. Be Concerned

"because many false prophets are gone out into the world."

1 John 5:3 "For this is the love of God, that we keep his commandments: and his commandments are not grievous."

I. The Endeavor

"the love of God"

II. The Entrance

"keep his commandments"

III. The Effort

"his commandments are not grievous"

I. The Work of the Savior

1 John 5:5 "Who is he that overcometh the world, but he that believeth that Jesus is the Son of God?"

II. The Witness of the Spirit

1 John 5:6 "This is he that came by water and blood, even Jesus Christ; not by water only, but by water and blood. And it is the Spirit that beareth witness, because the Spirit is truth."

III. The Word of the Sovereign

1 John 5:13 "These things have I written unto you that believe on the name of the Son of God; that ye may know that ye have eternal life, and that ye may believe on the name of the Son of God."

2 John 1:8 "Look to yourselves, that we lose not those things which we have wrought, but that we receive a full reward."

I. A Check Up

"Look to yourselves"

II. Before You Check Out

"that we lose not those things which we have wrought"

III. So You can Fully Check In

"but that we receive a full reward."

3 John 1:10 "Wherefore, if I come, I will remember his deeds which he doeth, prating against us with malicious words: and not content therewith, neither doth he himself receive the brethren, and forbiddeth them that would, and casteth them out of the church."

I. Trouble Makers cause Problems with their Conduct

"prating against us"

II. Trouble Makers cause Problems with their Conversation

"with malicious words"

III. Trouble Makers cause Problems with their Contentedness

"and not content therewith"

IV. Trouble Makers cause Problems with their Cliques

"neither doth he himself receive the brethren"

I. Compassion Ministry

Jude 1:22 "And of some have compassion, making a difference:"

II. Compelling Ministry

Jude 1:23 "And **others save with fear, pulling them out of the fire;** hating even the garment spotted by the flesh."

III. Clean Ministry

Jude 1:23 "And others save with fear, pulling them out of the fire; **hating even the garment spotted by the flesh.**"

Revelation 1:3 "Blessed is he that readeth, and they that hear the words of this prophecy, and keep those things which are written therein: for the time is at hand."

I. The Blessing of Studying Bible Prophecy

"Blessed is he that readeth, and they that hear the words of this prophecy"

II. The Benefit of Submitting to Bible Prophecy

"and keep those things which are written therein"

III. The Beauty of Searching Bible Prophecy

"for the time is at hand."

I. A Compliment from Christ

Revelation 2:2-3 "[2]I know thy works, and thy labour, and thy patience, and how thou canst not bear them which are evil: and thou hast tried them which say they are apostles, and are not, and hast found them liars: [3]And hast borne, and hast patience, and for my name's sake hast laboured, and hast not fainted."

II. A Complaint from Christ

Revelation 2:4 "Nevertheless I have somewhat against thee, because thou hast left thy first love."

III. A Correction from Christ

Revelation 2:5 "Remember therefore from whence thou art fallen, and repent, and do the first works; or else I will come unto thee quickly, and will remove thy candlestick out of his place, except thou repent."

Revelation 3:2 "Be watchful, and strengthen the things which remain, that are ready to die: for I have not found thy works perfect before God."

I. Focus on the Potential

"Be watchful"

II. Fix what's Possible

"strengthen the things which remain, that are ready to die:"

III. Fight for Perfection

"for I have not found thy works perfect before God."

Revelation 4:11 "Thou art worthy, O Lord, to receive glory and honour and power: for thou hast created all things, and for thy pleasure they are and were created."

I. The Greatness of Christ

"Thou art worthy"

II. The Glory of Christ

"to receive glory and honour and power"

III. The Galaxy of Christ

"for thou hast created all things"

IV. The Grandeur of Christ

"for thy pleasure they are and were created."

I. The Search

1 John 5:2-4 "And I saw a strong angel proclaiming with a loud voice, Who is worthy to open the book, and to loose the seals thereof? [3] And no man in heaven, nor in earth, neither under the earth, was able to open the book, neither to look thereon. [4] And I wept much, because no man was found worthy to open and to read the book, neither to look thereon."

II. The Savior

1 John 5:5-6 "And one of the elders saith unto me, Weep not: behold, the Lion of the tribe of Judah, the Root of David, hath prevailed to open the book, and to loose the seven seals thereof. [6] And I beheld, and, lo, in the midst of the throne and of the four beasts, and in the midst of the elders, stood a Lamb as it had been slain, having seven horns and seven eyes, which are the seven Spirits of God sent forth into all the earth."

III. The Supplication

1 John 5:8 "And when he had taken the book, the four beasts and four and twenty elders fell down before the Lamb, having every one of them harps, and golden vials full of odours, which are the prayers of saints."

III. The Singing

1 John 5:9 "And they sung a new song, saying, Thou art worthy to take the book, and to open the seals thereof: for thou wast slain, and hast redeemed us to God by thy blood out of every kindred, and tongue, and people, and nation;"

III. The Singers

1 John 5:11 "And I beheld, and I heard the voice of many angels round about the throne and the beasts and the elders: and the number of them was ten thousand times ten thousand, and thousands of thousands;"

1 John 5:13 "And every creature which is in heaven, and on the earth, and under the earth, and such as are in the sea, and all that are in them, heard I saying, Blessing, and honour, and glory, and power, be unto him that sitteth upon the throne, and unto the Lamb for ever and ever."

Revelation 6:17 "For the great day of his wrath is come; and who shall be able to stand?"

I. **The Coming Judgment**

"For the great day of his wrath is come"

II. **The Condemnation in Judgment**

"who shall be able to stand?"

I. **The First Seal-Peace**

Revelation 6:2 "And I saw, and behold a white horse: and he that sat on him had a bow; and a crown was given unto him: and he went forth conquering, and to conquer."

II. **The Second Seal-Provocations**

Revelation 6:4 "And there went out another horse that was red: and power was given to him that sat thereon to take peace from the earth, and that they should kill one another: and there was given unto him a great sword."

III. **The Third Seal-Poverty**

Revelation 6:5 "And when he had opened the third seal, I heard the third beast say, Come and see. And I beheld, and lo a black horse; and he that sat on him had a pair of balances in his hand."

IV. **The Fourth Seal-Plagues**

Revelation 6:8 "And I looked, and behold a pale horse: and his name that sat on him was Death, and Hell followed with him. And power was given unto them over the fourth part of the earth, to kill with sword, and with hunger, and with death, and with the beasts of the earth."

V. **The Fifth Seal-Persecution**

Revelation 6:9 "And when he had opened the fifth seal, I saw under the altar the souls of them that were slain for the word of God, and for the testimony which they held:"

VI. **The Sixth Seal-Pandemonium**

Revelation 6:12-13 "And I beheld when he had opened the sixth seal, and, lo, there was a great earthquake; and the sun became black as sackcloth of hair, and the moon became as blood; [13] And the stars of heaven fell unto the earth, even as a fig tree casteth her untimely figs, when she is shaken of a mighty wind."

Revelation 7:15 "Therefore are they before the throne of God, and serve him day and night in his temple: and he that sitteth on the throne shall dwell among them."

I. We'll Worship

"Therefore are they before the throne of God"

II. We'll Work

"and serve him day and night in his temple:"

III. We'll be With God

"and he that sitteth on the throne shall dwell among them."

Revelation 8:13 "And I beheld, and heard an angel flying through the midst of heaven, saying with a loud voice, Woe, woe, woe, to the inhabiters of the earth by reason of the other voices of the trumpet of the three angels, which are yet to sound!"

I. The Flight of the Angel

"and heard an angel flying through the midst of heaven"

II. The Force of the Angel

"saying with a loud voice"

III. The Fear of the Angel

"Woe, woe, woe, to the inhabiters of the earth"

Judgment is coming. Submit to Christ!

Revelation 9:6 "And in those days shall men seek death, and shall not find it; and shall desire to die, and death shall flee from them."

I. The Destruction in the Tribulation

"in those days"

II. The Desire in the Tribulation

"shall men seek death"

III. The Despair of the Tribulation

"and shall desire to die, and death shall flee from them."

Revelation 10:6 "And sware by him that liveth for ever and ever, who created heaven, and the things that therein are, and the earth, and the things that therein are, and the sea, and the things which are therein, that there should be time no longer:"

I. God is Continuous

"by him that liveth for ever and ever"

II. God is the Creator

"who created"

III. God is the Closer

"that there should be time no longer:"

Revelation 11:17 "Saying, We give thee thanks, O Lord God Almighty, which art, and wast, and art to come; because thou hast taken to thee thy great power, and hast reigned."

I. The Praise of God

"We give thee thanks, O Lord God Almighty"

II. The Permanence of God

"which art, and wast, and art to come"

III. The Power of God

"because thou hast taken to thee thy great power, and hast reigned."

Revelation 12:11 "And they overcame him by the blood of the Lamb, and by the word of their testimony; and they loved not their lives unto the death."

I. Their Support

"And they overcame him by the blood of the Lamb"

II. Their Statement

"and by the word of their testimony;"

III. Their Sacrifice

"and they loved not their lives unto the death."

I. The Rise of the Anti-Christ

A. It will be Supernatural

Revelation 13:1 "And I stood upon the sand of the sea, and saw a beast rise up out of the sea, having seven heads and ten horns, and upon his horns ten crowns, and upon his heads the name of blasphemy."

B. It will be Swift

Revelation 13:2 "And the beast which I saw was like unto a leopard, and his feet were as the feet of a bear, and his mouth as the mouth of a lion: and the dragon gave him his power, and his seat, and great authority."

II. The Reign of the Anti-Christ

Revelation 13:2-4 "And the beast which I saw was like unto a leopard, and his feet were as the feet of a bear, and his mouth as the mouth of a lion: and the dragon gave him his power, and his seat, and great authority. [3] And I saw one of his heads as it were wounded to death; and his deadly wound was healed: and all the world wondered after the beast. [4] And they worshipped the dragon which gave power unto the beast: and they worshipped the beast, saying, Who is like unto the beast? who is able to make war with him?"

III. The Ruin of the Anti-Christ-vs. 5-18

Revelation 14:13 "And I heard a voice from heaven saying unto me, Write, Blessed are the dead which die in the Lord from henceforth: Yea, saith the Spirit, that they may rest from their labours; and their works do follow them."

I. The Companion

"Blessed are the dead which die in the Lord"

II. The Comfort

"that they may rest from their labours;"

III. The Continuation

"and their works do follow them."

Revelation 15:4 "Who shall not fear thee, O Lord, and glorify thy name? for thou only art holy: for all nations shall come and worship before thee; for thy judgments are made manifest."

I. The Reverence of God

"Who shall not fear thee, O Lord"

II. The Recognition of God

"and glorify thy name?"

III. The Righteousness of God

"for thou only art holy"

IV. The Respect of God

"for all nations shall come and worship before thee;"

Revelation 16:5 "And I heard the angel of the waters say, Thou art righteous, O Lord, which art, and wast, and shalt be, because thou hast judged thus."

I. His Trustworthiness

"Thou art righteous, O Lord"

II. His Tenure

"which art, and wast, and shalt be,"

III. His Task

"thou hast judged thus"

Revelation 17:14 "These shall make war with the Lamb, and the Lamb shall overcome them: for he is Lord of lords, and King of kings: and they that are with him are called, and chosen, and faithful."

I. The Challenger

"These shall make war with the Lamb"

II. The Champion

"and the Lamb shall overcome them: for he is Lord of lords, and King of kings:"

III. The Companions

"and they that are with him are called, and chosen, and faithful."

I. The Separation from Sin

Revelation 18:4 "And I heard another voice from heaven, saying, Come out of her, my people, that ye be not partakers of her sins, and that ye receive not of her plagues."

I. The Significance of Sin

Revelation 18:5 "**For her sins have reached unto heaven,** and God hath remembered her iniquities."

II. The Seriousness of Sin

Revelation 18:5 "For her sins have reached unto heaven, and **God hath remembered her iniquities.**"

Revelation 19:11 "And I saw heaven opened, and behold a white horse; and he that sat upon him was called Faithful and True, and in righteousness he doth judge and make war."

I. The Coming of the King

"And I saw heaven opened, and behold a white horse;"

II. The Characteristics of the King

"he that sat upon him was called Faithful and True"

III. The Character of the King

"in righteousness"

IV. The Command of the King

"he doth judge and make war."

I. The Judge

Revelation 20:11 "And I saw a great white throne, **and him that sat on it,** from whose face the earth and the heaven fled away;"

II. The Judged

Revelation 20:12 "And I saw the dead, small and great, stand before God;"

III. The Judgment

Revelation 20:12 "...and **the dead were judged out of those things which were written in the books,** according to their works."

IV. The Justice

Revelation 20:12 "...and the dead were judged out of those things which were written in the books, **according to their works.**"

Revelation 21:7 "He that overcometh shall inherit all things; and I will be his God, and he shall be my son."

I. The Reward

"He that overcometh shall inherit all things"

II. The Relationship

"and I will be his God"

III. The Responsibility

"and he shall be my son."

I. The River in that City

Revelation 22:1 "And he shewed me a **pure river of water** of life, clear as crystal, proceeding out of the throne of God and of the Lamb."

II. The Refreshment in that City

Revelation 22:2 "In the midst of the street of it, and on either side of the river, was **there the tree of life,** which bare twelve manner of fruits, and yielded her fruit every month: and the leaves of the tree were for the healing of the nations."

III. The Ruler of that City

Revelation 22:3 "And there shall be no more curse: but **the throne of God** and of the Lamb shall be in it; and his servants shall serve him:"

IV. The Relationships in that City

Revelation 22:4 "And **they shall see his face;** and his name shall be in their foreheads."

V. The Radiance of that City

Revelation 22:5 "And **there shall be no night there;** and they need no candle, neither light of the sun; for the Lord God giveth them light: and they shall reign for ever and ever."